SUSTAINING

Heaven

ON

Earth

Keys Forged By and For Love

ISAURA BARRERA

BALBOA.PRESS
A DIVISION OF HAY HOUSE

Balboa Press books may be ordered through booksellers or by contacting:

Balboa Press
A Division of Hay House
1663 Liberty Drive
Bloomington, IN 47403
www.balboapress.com
844-682-1282

All Scripture quotations are taken from THE MESSAGE, copyright © 1993, 2002, 2018 by Eugene H. Peterson. Used by permission of NavPress. All rights reserved. Represented by Tyndale House Publishers, Inc.

Print information available on the last page.

ISBN: 978-1-9822-7240-1 (sc)
ISBN: 978-1-9822-7241-8 (hc)
ISBN: 978-1-9822-7239-5 (e)

Library of Congress Control Number: 2021915487

Balboa Press rev. date: 08/09/2021

DEDICATION

As always, to my beloved friend

ACKNOWLEDGMENTS

I want to acknowledge Victoria, Joel and Christyan, the Oblate School of Theology Continuing Education staff who made it possible for me to offer a course on sustaining heaven on earth. Your warm and welcoming spirit allowed me to share my ideas with greater confidence. Your technological support allowed me to share them more skillfully and smoothly than I might have otherwise.

I also want to acknowledge all the students in that course whose enthusiastic participation helped me to both refine and expand my initial ideas. Thank you so much for your kind reception of my words. I am particularly grateful to the students who volunteered to serve as beta readers for my initial manuscript.

Finally, I want to acknowledge all those, met and unmet, whose words brought me both inspiration and insight. These include all the writers listed in the Book Providence of this book as well as others met in person and through Face Book posts.

TABLE OF CONTENTS

AUTHOR'S NOTE

An anonymous quote I once read came to mind as I started to write this book: "Please excuse the inefficiency of my work. The nature of it requires such a high degree of complexity that I simply don't know what I'm doing."[1] The task I have undertaken in writing this book requires something different yet equally daunting: a radical simplicity of such depth that its mystery cannot truly be addressed with any clarity. Or perhaps radical simplicity is merely the underside of complexity. Whatever the case, I ask you to bear with me as I dare to address the task before me: an exploration of four keys to sustaining heaven on earth forged by and for a love I never expected or imagined.

The content in this book is rooted in the lived experience of that love, which changed me even as it returned me home. Writing about that experience has both affirmed and deepened that return. I share what I've learned now in the belief that the value of others' stories is "not to tell us how or whether to proceed."[2] It is, rather, to create "a space of engagement" within which readers can find hope and inspiration for themselves.

I hope that I have done my work of creating such a space well. To whatever degree I have not done so, "Please excuse the inefficiency of my work."

INTRODUCTION

Heaven on earth is a reality that defies description and even belief at times. Yet all who have fallen in love, felt deep wonder, or witnessed what could only be classified as a miracle can attest to its presence. Unfortunately, that presence is all too often only fleeting, an experience that leaves us awaiting the next extraordinary event. What if it didn't have to be so? What if it was possible to sustain the experience of heaven on earth?

This book suggests four keys to doing so, each forged by and for a love that first re-awakened me to heaven on earth and then challenged me to remain awake to its presence. Part I overviews the twofold context within which the keys were forged: an adventure of love and my understanding of heaven on earth. The adventure of love on which I found myself was first and foremost the driving force behind forging the keys. It was through that adventure that heaven on earth became concrete for me, something beyond anything I'd imagined I'd ever experience, something to be sustained.

Part II devotes a chapter to each key starting with a discussion of my understanding of that key as it was forged through my adventure and followed by a scripturally based reflection associated with that understanding. A brief overview of selected practices that I found supportive of the key is also included along with a section titled Book Providence, which identifies significant books from which I drew information and inspiration related to the key. Each aspect—discussion, scriptural reflection, practices, and Book Providence—provides one piece of the whole from which, or perhaps through which, the keys emerged. Additionally, Appendix II provides questions for exploring each key in more depth.

Part III, After Thoughts, encompasses several reflections on living a heaven on earth sustained. These reflections, outgrowths of the four keys, remain unfinished, as do the understandings that have given them birth. They provide only hints of what will draw me next as my adventure of love continues.

Part I

CONTEXT

I remember when I was first recalled into a love I'd stopped believing could really be. Heaven come to earth! How could I not follow? I didn't look back then, not until I started to stumble across new ground with no familiar paths and love opened long locked doors.
(I. Barrera)

ontext: "that which forms the setting for an event, statement or idea and in terms of which it can be fully understood and accessed."[3] The context within which the four keys addressed in this book were forged was twofold: heart-based and experiential as well as mind-based and conceptual.

Chapter 1 addresses the heart-based experiential context: my unexpected adventure of love. This heart-based experiential context is in many ways the most pivotal. Though detailed in another book,[4] its role vis-à-vis the forging of keys is too significant to not mention in this one.

Chapter II focuses on the more mind-based and conceptual component of the context within which the keys were forged. Its focus is on the definition and description of the heaven on earth to which I awakened through my adventure of love. This chapter addresses my thoughts and understandings of that heaven on earth, which were concretized as I sought to inform my heart-based intuitions more broadly through reading and study.

Mind and heart together are essential, visible creation and invisible reality. In some ways, this twofold context parallels that of heaven on earth. Heaven is, after all, an invisible and ultimately un-provable reality best accessed through the heart's intuition while earth is a proven reality easily accessible with the mind's logic and reason.

A DARING ADVENTURE
OF LOVE

*Life ... should be a daring adventure of
love—a continuous journey of putting aside
our securities to enter more profoundly
into the uncharted depths of God.*
(Ilia Delio)

*A*ll of us, I believe, live daring adventures of love. Whether
we recognize them as such or not, whether defined by love's
apparent absence or its undeniable presence, life's uncharted
depths both challenge and extend an invitation to us all to enter
into an adventure of love. Whatever we name them, depths of life
or depths of God, their reality remains unchanged.

If these statements resonate for you, then come share my
reflections on my own daring adventure of love. Harvest from
them whatever may help you on yours.

My adventure started long before I was aware of what was
happening. Perhaps its roots were grounded in my reading of
the gospels as love stories. Accounts of practical, hard-working
and apparently sensible men and women dropping everything
to follow someone they've just met have always been, for me,
reminiscent of love at first sight scenarios. How else could they be
explained? I have always thought that these men and women were
motivated by what I, and so many others, yearn for so deeply:
"a sense of gifted love so strong and so deep it literally brings

heaven to earth, making sacredness and miracles as palpable as trees and cats."[5]

Spiritual mystics across the centuries have written of such love. One such was St. John of the Cross, a 16th century Spanish Christian mystic. He laid out its path in unforgettable poetry whose words stirred my heart when I first read them long before my own adventure started. I found one of his poems particularly inspiring in relation to my adventure.

ONE DARK NIGHT[6]

One dark night
With love-inflamed yearning,
O wondrous adventure!
I set out unseen
My house now still at last.

Surely, in the dark,
Disguised, I left by the secret ladder
O joyous adventure!
In the dark and watchful
My house now still at last.

On that wondrous night
In secret, no one saw me
And I saw no one,
Without other light or guide
but for the fire in my heart.

Guided by that fire
More certainly than the brightest sun at noon
To where waited whom I well knew
There, where there was no one.

O guiding night!
O night warmer than the dawn!
O night that united beloved with Beloved
beloved into Beloved transformed!

On my flowering breast
That wholly I kept for my Beloved alone
There my Beloved remained sleeping
And I loved,
while cedars fanned the air.

Wind through the castle battlements
As I ran my fingers through his hair,
With his gentle hand
On my neck he pierced my soul
And all my faculties suspended.

I stayed, self forgotten,
Reclining my face on my Beloved,
All ceased and I left myself
Leaving all care and concern
There, strewn among the lilies.

As I re-read the poem at the beginning of my adventure, its echo in the apostles' response to Jesus was unmistakable. Only such love, I felt, could provide the courage to leave all care and concern behind and live as they and all the saints I'd read about had lived—as I, in all the innocence and fervor of childhood, yearned to live yet never dreamed I could or would.

My Own Daring Adventure
of Love—Then

My daring adventure of love first appeared on the horizon over two decades ago when I reconnected with a long lost friend and fell in love with him once again.[7] It was, as all true love is, heaven on earth.[8] As the first glow of our renewed friendship began to fade, however, the challenge of sustaining that heaven on earth emerged front and center. While my friend was physically present here on earth, my tendency was always to turn toward him in response to that challenge. Even as I recognized its spiritual aspects, I remained focused on the path of our human relationship.

Toward the end of what I now realize was only the first half of my adventure, I became more and more aware that sustaining heaven on earth had never been truly defined solely along a chronological timeline walked with a human beloved. Its essence always had been, and continues to be, most deeply defined along a spiritual timeline walked with a Divine Beloved as well as a human beloved now in spirit. What had been background became foreground with my friend's passing.

My Own Daring Adventure
of Love—Now

The challenge to sustaining heaven on earth deepened in the absence of my friend's physical presence and reassurances. As I strived to sustain the heaven on earth I'd found with him during his life on earth I realized that keys essential to sustaining it even in his physical absence had been being forged all along. Paradoxically, it was the very twist and turns that challenged that sustaining that simultaneously fueled their forging. I began to increasingly ponder sustaining heaven on earth as something beyond and greater than the joy and wonder my friend and I experienced in each other's presence.

For a long time, the keys that had been being forged remained largely intuitive. They developed organically and only emerged clearly after my friend's passing as I began to intentionally reflect on sustaining heaven on earth as the vibrant and living reality to which he had awakened me through his physical presence.

The keys are at the core of my adventure now, deeper gift beneath and beyond the gift of the unimagined and unimaginable friendship my beloved friend offered me. They continue to be further forged and together allow me to both sustain heaven on earth and participate in its continuing co-creation.

I invite you to explore the keys with me in the hope that they will help you unfold your own daring adventure of love and sustain a heaven on earth beyond your wildest dreams, be it in relation to a human beloved or in relation to whatever life situations you are living.

HEAVEN ON EARTH

*At the heart of our being is the image of God and
thus the wisdom of God, the creativity of God,
the passions of God, the longings of God.*
(J. P. Newell)

"Heaven on earth:" just what is it that I am proposing can be sustained with the four keys I identify? Heaven on earth is a phrase whose meaning most of us believe we know yet which we can never truly define. A Spanish saying comes to mind when I consider how to talk about my understanding of heaven on earth: *Cada cabeza un mundo.*[9] It reminds me that words are not reality; they are only symbols that represent reality. Their meaning, like that of all symbols, lies in what is attributed to them in each of our minds rather than in any objective reality.[10] Their meanings come alive only in the subjective context of our experiences.

The following paragraphs are not intended to be complete or definitive descriptions in relation to either heaven on earth as some absolute reality or to heaven on earth as my own subjective personal experience. They are only intended to provide a general sense of how I've come and am still coming to understand both.

For me, the meaning of the words *heaven on earth* comes alive within the subjective context of my experiences of joy, peace, love, hope, wonder, and awe amid confusion, doubt, fear and dreams unfulfilled. While these experiences do not define heaven on earth in any objective way, they do evoke a sense of it for me as a space where divine consciousness and human experience meet, discernible within yet also simultaneously beyond the limitations of human experience. Heaven on earth becomes a palpable reality when I experience joy and dreams fulfilled. While the reverse—the absence of joy and dreams unfulfilled—did not at first yield the same sense of heaven on earth, its presence even then started to become palpable as I committed to sustaining it.

I did not and do not think that I reach any ideal or perfect reality through my experiences. I do believe that through them I touch the edges of an Infinite Light and Love greater than any I ever imagined possible in this life. It is those edges, which I continue to explore, that for me are heaven on earth.

QUALITIES OF HEAVEN ON EARTH

The deep joy, wonder, light and love I found with my beloved friend evoked *heaven on earth* for me.[11] Three qualities borrowed from Booram and Booram's[12] discussion of "when the heavens open" capture my sense of what I experienced, which continues to be core to my understanding.

The first of these qualities is a shift from *chronos* or clock time to *kairos* or timelessness. When I experienced moments of what I believed must be heaven on earth, my awareness of chronological time fell into the background or, at times, disappeared all together. I experienced "seeing beyond temporal time into the ways things are in eternity."[13]

I remember feeling frustrated, for example, at the beginning of my adventure when my friend would call and say he had only two or three minutes to talk. Just as I was settling into our conversation, it would be time to stop and say goodbye. Sometimes I even felt that it might be better not to talk at all. Then one day, after we'd only talked for a few minutes, I realized

I'd lost all track of time. We had only talked for a few minutes yet it had felt like hours. I'd lost all sense of time or incompleteness as I immersed myself in the joy, love and light his presence stirred up in me. That sense of timelessness continues to be one I consider intrinsic to my experience of heaven on earth.

The second quality Booram and Booram associate with heaven on earth is "a heightened awareness of ...*sheer magnitude*." It did not take long for me to become aware that my experience of my friend's love and the joy that accompanied that love encompassed so much more than I had ever imagined or believed possible. I knew without a doubt that here was something endless. Here was something whose magnitude exceeded anything I had ever known or could ever imagine. My sense of heaven on earth as beyond human creation and human limits was and is an important aspect of my recognition of it as heaven on earth.

My experience of magnitude brought with it an intuition of *mystery*, the third quality of heaven on earth identified by Booram and Booram. Not only did I sense that here was something endless, I also knew that here was something that could not be explained or accounted for in any logical fashion. I could neither know nor imagine why my friend loved me as he did or inspired the response that he did. There was no logic to our relationship. In fact, in many ways our relationship simply made no sense. We lived in different places, spoke only a few times a month and often miscommunicated more than communicated. Yet, the mystery of our friendship only deepened when I allowed it to be. It was a mystery that I could experience yet that was not mine to achieve, control and possess.

Timelessness, magnitude, and mystery: three qualities that for me have come to define heaven on earth. They are qualities affirmed by Christian mystics such St. John of the Cross and St. Teresa of Avila as well as more recent spiritual writers (e.g., Ilia

Delio, Richard Rohr, Cynthia Bourgeault) as they point to the ability of humans to experience heaven while still here on earth. Interestingly, while other more secular writers do not speak of heaven on earth, some of what they say seems curiously analogous. One example comes from Philip M. Lewis as he discusses Stage 5, the highest stage of psychological development as described by Robert Kegan, a Harvard psychologist.[14] As he points out that the explanation of this stage might be a bit fuzzy, he also states "…I suspect you'll do better if you look for descriptions of what may be Stage 5 in the writings of some of the religious mystics."[15]

HEAVEN ON EARTH IS ABOUT HOW, NOT WHERE, WE ARE

My image of heaven on earth is not about a place. Where I was when I experienced the deep joy, peace, love, hope, wonder, and awe that signaled heaven's presence on earth for me never seemed to matter. What always did matter was *how* I was (e.g., open or shut down, angry or confused). If, for example, I was frustrated or otherwise upset, even the longest conversation with my friend did not feel timeless. If, on the other hand, I was at peace, the shortest conversation seemed eternal.

I believe heaven is not some *where*. It is in the depth of *here*, a state of being defined by Infinite Light and Love.[16] Unfortunately, much of what is written about heaven all too often comes from the perspective of it as a place. There has consequently been an emphasis on getting to heaven rather than living heaven on earth. It almost seems at times that the whole purpose of spiritual endeavors is to get to heaven rather than, as one writer puts it, "to get heaven in you."[17] Heaven is treated as object, a reality or concept apart from us that we can "have." As subject, in contrast, heaven is a state of being in which we are immersed and with which we are intimately entangled.

In my own adventure it did not take long to realize that I could have what I experienced as heaven on earth with my friend or I could simply be *in* that heaven on earth. When I saw heaven on earth as something I could have, it became an object, something somehow separate from me that I could step out of to judge or assess and compare to what I believed it should or could be.

When instead I was *in* heaven on earth I could simply allow it to be, without judgment or assessment. I did not fear its loss and did not need to guard against it. I could simply *be*, recognizing that it was in the depth of *here* where I could sink into it than stepping out of it to judge or assess its presence.

HEAVEN AND EARTH ARE COMPLEMENTARY

My image of heaven on earth is one in which heaven and earth cannot *be* without each other. They are complementary rather than contradictory, intertwined aspects of a single reality like contrasting colors on a single spectrum. Heaven's energy resides deep within earth's realities while earth's realities *"simultaneously ...* pierce the heart of God."[18]

To separate heaven (i.e., love, beauty, awe, wonder) from earth's trials is "to lose the personal intimacy" of God's infinite self playing through the chords of my being. To separate earth's trials from heaven is to "lose the cosmic vastness" of God [Infinite Light and Love], within which their sting can be softened. Only together can earth's flawed and limited notes echo "within the glory and birth pangs of the universe," and vice versa."[19]

Sufi tradition has a lovely metaphor that reflects this understanding: "where the two seas meet." It is a metaphor for where one is "caught in the currents of the ocean of divine consciousness and yet also held in the sea of human experience."[20] Coming from a tradition very different from Christianity, these words nevertheless capture the intimate complementarity of heaven and earth for me.

HEAVEN ON EARTH CANNOT BE TRULY IMAGED

It is somewhat ironic to talk about my image of heaven on earth when a major aspect of that image is that heaven on earth cannot truly be imaged. Experiences of joy, love, awe and wonder can hint of its shape and presence but cannot truly define it. Though complementary to earth's three-dimensional reality and accessible to us while here on earth, heaven remains hidden beyond the scope of our ordinary earth-grounded senses and faculties.

In his renowned work, *Dark Night of the Soul*, St. John of the Cross identifies two types of barriers that keep heaven (i.e., union with God, in his words) hidden from earth. The first barrier is the barrier created by the limitations of our physical senses (e.g. sight, hearing, touch). Perceiving heaven requires stepping beyond what our senses can tell us is real. It requires, for example, learning to know love is present and real even when the signs we believe prove its presence are absent (e.g., we don't get the call we believe would prove its presence). We may seldom hear the words "I love you" and yet be deeply loved. Similarly, heaven on earth may not seem to be present and yet be all around us.

The second type of barrier to perceiving heaven on earth is a subtler one. It is the barrier created by the limitations of what, in keeping with the culture of his time, St. John called our faculties: intellect, will and memory. Heaven on earth can never truly be grasped by our intellect. Our intellect cannot prove its existence no matter how deep or complex our thoughts. What we can understand or apprehend with our intellect is but a small part of reality.[21]

Similarly, the perception and experience of heaven on earth lie beyond the capacity of our will to produce. Though we may have the illusion of control, we cannot will ourselves to perceive or experience heaven on earth no matter how hard we try. We cannot will the reality of Infinite Light and Love anymore than we can will another to love us.

Memory, tied as it is to only what has defined reality for us in the past, is equally incapable of producing the perception or experience of heaven on earth. Memory cannot produce a living heaven on earth; it can only present us with past images and experiences of heaven on earth. Reflecting on the limitations of memory to keep my experience of heaven on earth fresh and responsive to the present became especially important for me after my friend passed.

I could remember heaven on earth as I'd known it in his presence, as it no longer was. Yet what I needed to learn was to re-member so that it would still be present. Remembering is a function of memory. It involves recalling previous experience that are no longer present. Re-membering transcends that function. It involves bringing back to wholeness in such a way that what was still is.[22] The meaning of re-membering is closer to invoking than to recalling.[23] The difference is subtle yet significant. When we remember heaven on earth we box it into the images generated by our memory and render it no longer accessible. When we re-member heaven on earth we invoke or call it forth as reality that remains present and accessible.[24]

From a modern contemporary perspective, one could say that heaven on earth is hidden behind or beyond what Deepak Chopra calls the virtual reality created by our senses and faculties.[25] My adventure led me beyond that virtual reality by refusing to conform to it and challenging me to seek a deeper reality. I discovered that defining the reality of heaven on earth according to my senses and my faculties repeatedly locked me out of heaven on earth as a lived experience.

Believing, for example, that what I felt or thought (e.g., he didn't call so he no longer cares; we had a wonderful time, this must be heaven on earth) was absolute actually diminished my experience of heaven on earth or erased it altogether. Believing that being together with my beloved was a reality now accessible only as a memory, did the same. When, instead, I remained committed to my relationship with my friend and opened to what lay hidden behind or beyond my feelings, thoughts, and memories, my experience of heaven on earth returned and deepened. It was that experience, independent of time, space and the limitations of human senses and faculties that I sought to sustain.

Part II
KEYS

There are times when, in moments of insight—sudden openings of the heart—we glimpse once again the mysterious reality we took for granted as children
(I. Barrera)

While my beloved friend was physically present, my experience of his love made my experience of heaven on earth concrete and palpable. After his passing, I feared that my experience heaven on earth would be diminished. Paradoxically, with that fear came the intuition that keys to sustaining heaven on earth as a concrete and palpable experience had been being forged all along as I walked the path carved out by the adventure of love we shared.

Developed organically rather than intentionally or sequentially, the keys remained largely intuitive and unconscious for a long time, their patterns becoming clear only in hindsight. My description of them in the following pages is therefore neither purely objective nor abstract. Both memory and cognitive reconstruction of past experience shape what I say about each as much as does my growing understanding and awareness as they continue to help me sustain an ever more present heaven on earth.

The first key I discuss, *choosing heaven on earth*, began to be forged during times when things did not go well (according to my judgment) and I struggled to reconnect with the heaven on earth that was so evident when things did go well. It was further forged and strengthened after my friend's passing when his physical absence challenged me even more strongly to affirm the heaven on earth I'd come to know in his presence.

The second key—*deepening love, hope and faith*—was progressively forged as I came to and somehow surpassed—or at least refused to be imprisoned by—the limits of my love, hope and faith. Times when my love seemed too weak to survive without the assurances on which I'd come to depend, for example, pushed me to deepen my love. Times that depleted my hope in things ever changing pushed me to find a deeper hope. Times when my faith was taken to its limits similarly served to stoke the forging of a deeper faith.

The third key, *seeing with binocular vision*, began to take form as I struggled with apparent contradictions between what I believed was heaven on earth and what I could only recognize as "not-heaven on earth." It was shaped as I struggled to see both simultaneously without needing to erase one in favor of the other.

The regular use of these first three keys gradually led to the forging of a fourth: *reading life as sacred text*. Though dependent on the first three, this last key became a master key. It first began to take shape as I learned to seek and read the greater spiritual reality that underlay all the details of the wondrous friendship given me. Paradoxically, it remained largely intuitive the longest, not becoming conscious or intentional until I reacquainted myself with the Christian practice of *lectio divina*.[26] That practice laid the groundwork for reading my life as sacred text consciously and intentionally.

Inspired and cultivated through my beloved friend's presence, both physical and spiritual, the keys have become the deeper gift beneath and beyond the gift of the unimagined and unimaginable love and friendship he offered me. I share each now in the spirit of a postcard sent to say, "Look what I've found! Come and see for yourself."

Of course I can't prove that what I've learned to sustain is really heaven on earth in any absolute sense. I can only say that it's an accessible and wondrous reality that enlivens and enriches my life in ways I only imagined possible before finding it.

CHOOSING HEAVEN
ON EARTH

*"Whatever is true, whatever is honorable, whatever
is fair, whatever is pure, whatever is commendable, if
there is anything of excellence and if there is anything
praise worthy, keep thinking about these things."*
(Philippians 4:8)

When my connection with my beloved friend unfolded in ways that brought me joy and feelings of being deeply cherished, I had no doubt I was in heaven on earth. When my connection did not unfold as I thought it could or should those feelings dissolved. Like clouds hiding all sight of the sun, doubt and hopelessness erased my heaven on earth. Yet I could not bear what I believed to be its loss. No matter what happened, I decided to choose to believe that every moment offered me the gift of heaven on earth, only waiting for me to unwrap and explore it.

It was at those times that what I later recognized as the first key to sustaining heaven on earth, *choosing heaven on earth*, began to be forged, albeit only intuitively.

As I sought to rise above the clouds of doubt and hopelessness I discovered that choosing heaven on earth was, ultimately, about choosing to keep an open heart in the face of experiences that disturbed and clouded my vision. Three types of experiences presented me with the greatest obstacles. Paradoxically they also provided the greatest incentive to keeping an open heart.

The first type of experience was the experience of being between where I wanted to be and where I was (e.g., between feeling totally in harmony with my friend and feeling no longer loved and at odds with him). As I began to explore these experiences I realized that they were not endings but rather thresholds from one relational, spiritual or simply experiential territory to another.

A second more challenging type of experience was the experience of dark nights when things stopped making sense and heaven on earth seemed nowhere to be found. Sometimes an experience of a dark night was triggered as I found myself at a threshold. Most times, however, it seemed to come suddenly, apparently out of nowhere.

Finally, and unexpectedly, the experience of "bright" days, when everything seemed especially wondrous and perfect, also challenged my ability to keep an open heart as I clung to them. Each type of experience brought with it its own distinct challenge and contribution to shaping the first key to sustaining heaven on earth.

THRESHOLDS

When I found myself between what I recognized as heaven on earth and what seemed to be anything but heaven on earth, there seemed to no longer be a heaven on earth to choose. How could I choose what seemed so obviously absent? How could I keep my heart open to what no longer seemed to be present? It was not as simple as changing my thoughts. To move through and beyond thresholds I needed to shift my energy so as to once again allow myself to experience the lightness and joy of heaven on earth even in the absence of what I believed to be evidence of its presence.

I remembered thresholds I'd experienced before. Looking back at those times, I recognized that they had pushed me out of the boxes into which I thought my future would fit and prodded me to realize that heaven on earth was still there. Crossing the threshold from deep loneliness into a renewed friendship, for example, was a threshold experience that led me into a heaven on earth I neither imagined nor anticipated. Before I reconnected with my beloved friend, the positive future I yearned for seemed to be increasingly slipping from a not-here-now space into a not-here-ever space. Aware of a discomfort with where I was and a haunting hopelessness that what I'd wished for so long would never come I could not imagine what lay ahead as anything other than a continuation of the "not enough" life I'd lived so far.

Over time I realized that thresholds are not the empty spaces they seemed to be. They are gestational spaces, holding me until I could step beyond my desperate yearning for a specific outcome into a heaven on earth bigger than that outcome. Perhaps the secret of keeping an open heart (i.e., choosing heaven on earth) while seemingly stuck at a threshold is to recognize the paradox that lies at its core: "...the mystery of a new beginning out of what looks like death."[27]

As I felt the dying of long-held dreams and expectations at each threshold, I discovered the beginning of something that was, in fact, the fulfillment of those very dreams and expectations in unimagined form. Now, when experiencing myself at a threshold, I remember to choose the heaven on earth it carries though yet unfolded.

DARK NIGHTS[28]

A second type of experience that proved to be both obstacle and opportunity to choosing heaven on earth was the experience of what St. John of the Cross calls "dark nights," times when I lost sight of that on which I relied to navigate and negotiate my life.[29] I repeatedly fell into these when, for example, my relationship with my friend seemed to reach the limits—the finitude—of anything I could place into a familiar or comprehensible framework.

Cynthia Bourgeault provides an apt analogy for such times in one of her books.[30] Unlike sailing on a bright day when we can be guided by what we can see ahead, when sailing in a fog we can no longer see what lies ahead. It is then, she points out, that we must pay careful attention to where we are. Ironically, it was when I felt "in a fog," that I least wanted to pay attention to where I was. Yet, Bourgeault continues, that is precisely where we need to put our attention. When sailing in a fog we must find our way "by being sensitively and sensuously connected to exactly where you are… responding to subtle intimations of presence too delicate to pick up at [the] normal level of awareness."[31]

It took a long time and many struggles before I learned to open my heart sufficiently to "sensitively and sensuously" connect to heaven on earth as it was rather than as I wished it to be. Each time I did, though, I discovered the truth of something I'd once read but had not understood: "When every pain, every separation, is allowed to remain—that is, to exist in its fullness of feeling—then the light it is made of [i.e., its miracle] begins to emerge."[32]

I wrote the following as I emerged from one dark night: "…I believe that these times happen because only the depth of the unwavering commitment they stimulate can ensure that heaven (Infinite Light and Love) and earth (all we hold dear) remain one no matter what."[33] It is more important than we know, literally, to sustain an unwavering commitment to choosing heaven on earth in the midst of dark nights.

Ironically, dark nights have now become the most rewarding times for me (though often they are still the most difficult and frustrating). I have learned and continue to learn to trust that unimagined vistas that could not be revealed any other way will open up as each night dissolves into day.

Bright days

The third type of experience that challenged my commitment to choosing heaven on earth was an unexpected one: bright days. At first I did not expect bright days to present any challenge. After all, it was on those days that I felt the presence of heaven on earth most strongly. It almost seemed as if it chose me.

Sailing on bright days has many advantages that disguise their challenge. As a song says, "On a clear day, you can see forever." Over time, however, I discovered that with that seemingly endless sight came two temptations. The first was to grasp the heaven on earth bright days revealed too tightly and resist sight of it in any other form. The second was to give in to the fear that bright days are "too good to be true" and consequently not truly choose the heaven on earth they reveal.

On many bright days, I would cling desperately to the joy they revealed, fearful it would disappear. On others, caution would keep me guarded, afraid to grasp their full reality lest it be only an illusion. Both clinging and fearful caution blocked choosing heaven on earth on bright days as surely as during thresholds and dark nights.

My struggles through thresholds, dark nights and the temptations of bright days shaped the forging of the first key to sustaining heaven on earth. I still remember the first time I consciously and intentionally chose heaven on earth when it seemed to be gone. It was literally as well as experientially a dark night. My friend and I had just talked. Something had not gone as I'd expected and I felt I was losing him. In the middle of my "dark" feelings I found myself suddenly asking, "Why am I not allowing myself to choose heaven on earth in this darkness?" "Am I misguidedly trying to protect its light by keeping it apart from the darkness I feel" "Am I afraid there is no longer any light to protect?"

Unexpectedly, just asking the questions changed everything. I realized that what I'd believed to be an immutable absence of heaven on earth was actually a self-imposed choice. I discovered I could choose to shift my energy and feel heaven on earth even in the midst of what I was sure was its absence! My feelings of loss, fear and depression did not disappear, yet there, right alongside them, I found feelings of joy and peace that signaled the presence of heaven on earth.

There is a story told about the Jewish Rabbi Baal Shem-Tov that highlighted for me the importance of this commitment to choosing heaven on earth no matter the circumstances.[34] This Rabbi, it is said, regularly averted any misfortune threatening his community by going to pray at a special place in a nearby forest. There, he would light a fire, say a special prayer and all would be well. After his death, one of his disciples continued his practice. Though he did not know how to light the fire, this disciple knew the place and the special prayer, and that was enough. All would once again be well.

The following generation's rabbi could not remember either how to light the fire or the magic prayer that needed to be said. He could only remember the place, and he continued to go there. Surprisingly, that was once again enough. The succeeding rabbi could not even remember the place. He could only say: "I am unable to light the fire and I do not know the prayer; I cannot even find the place in the forest. All I can do is ask You to redeem us, and this must be sufficient." And, the story says, that was sufficient.

This story helped me to remember that choosing heaven on earth is first and foremost about affirming the commitment to stay connected to Infinite Light and Love in all circumstances and at all times. That is always enough.

Scripture Reflection

*Steep your life in God-reality, God-
initiative, God-provisions*
(Matthew 6:33, *The Message*)

First things first. Follow me. Pursue life
(Matthew 8:22, *The Message*)

As always in my journey, I believed I could find resonance for my experiences in the scripture story, which for me has always been about an adventure of love.[35] I continued to seek that resonance now. In that story choosing heaven on earth—steeping our life in "God reality, God initiative and God-provisions"—is put in a relational context with two words: "Follow me."

I imagined those words spoken directly to me. I felt them more than heard them. They resonated from within me rather than coming from without:

As I turned toward you my heart stirred, as it had not in a very long time. I felt I'd found heaven on earth. I wanted to follow you so that I'd never lose it. Yet you gave no destination; just those words "Follow me."

I wondered "Follow you where?" "Follow you how?" "Where is this heaven on earth you awaken in me?" You gave no destination, no location; just those words "Follow me."

It took time for me to begin to understand that following you was not about going to a destination or a place. It was not a means to an end at all, though I'd first understood it as such. It was not directional at all. It was an end in itself, defined by *how* I went and *how* I was, not by where I went or where I was. The more I turned toward you and steeped myself in the heaven on earth I found with you, the more I realized that there was no place to go; there was only <u>here</u> to be. Following you was not about going anywhere; it was about falling in love for the sheer joy and adventure of finding myself embraced by love in return.

As long as I remained aware of that, the steps necessary to follow you appeared without effort or forethought, like the movement of branches in response to the wind that swirls around them. They do not choose the direction or form of their movements, they only choose to remain responsive to the wind.

Selected Practices to Support Choosing Heaven on Earth

As I discovered that choosing heaven on earth was key to sustaining my experience of it, I also discovered that it did not always happen spontaneously. At it core lay an energetic shift that involved opening my heart to reconnect with Infinite Light and Love in a palpable way. I began to seek ways of opening my heart to its presence more intentionally. I found three practices in particular that were helpful.

The first was a practice of re-membering rather than merely remembering my experiences of heaven on earth. The act of remembering (with no hyphen) involves seeing through the lens of memory, recalling what is no longer present as it used to be. It is a movement into the past. In contrast, the act of re-membering (with a hyphen) is a movement in the present. It involves reconstituting what no longer appears to be whole, entering into its reality as still present and living. There is, after all, no time in heaven on earth. Re-membering my experiences of heaven on earth, entering into them as a living reality, sustained heaven on earth in the present for me.

A second more formalized practice I found useful is one I adapted from the tradition of liturgical hours. That tradition is an ancient Christian practice within which the chronological hours of the day are understood as "messengers of eternity in the natural flow of time" [36] and are observed with specific prayers. In adapting that tradition, I interpreted "hours" non-chronologically, shifting my focus from clock hours to more metaphorical times (e.g., light on the horizon, full light, lamp-lighting time). I'd start by discerning what time best matched my experience at a particular time. Was I, for example, at a time when I could sense light on the horizon as if at dawn? Was I sensing a growing light of inspiration or understanding on the horizon? Or, regardless of the hour on the clock, did I feel I was in a time more like midnight, with little light to be seen? After discerning the time that best matched my experience, I would then meditate on it using material from *Music of Silence* by Steidl-Rast & Lebell and *sevensacredpauses* by Macrina Wiedekehr. (See Appendix I for specific information on the hours as I adapted and interpreted them)

Sometimes, though, I'd find that I could not choose heaven on earth directly. That was when I was drawn to a third practice. My practice then was to choose to be willing. Like the Jewish descendants of Rabbi Baal Shem-Tov all I could do was hold the intent to choose heaven on earth. At those times I found that the hour did not matter nearly as much as my willingness to connect with Infinite Light and Love.

BOOK PROVIDENCE[37]

No one travels adventures of love alone, and I certainly didn't. I am indebted to the writings of multiple writers for their insights on the constancy of heaven on earth during thresholds, dark nights and bright days. The following books are some that I found insightful:

Rohlheiser, R. *Against an Infinite Horizon: The Finger of God in Our Everyday Lives*. This book affirmed my sense that heaven could indeed be found on earth even when our images of it fail to reflect it.

Shulman, J. *The Instruction Manual for Receiving God*. Reading this book brought me the insight that it is not heaven on earth but ourselves that need to be unlocked so that we can receive Infinite Light and Love.

Ryan, S. *Praying Dangerously: Radical Reliance on God*. The words in this book supported my realization that choosing heaven on earth was about a radical reliance that repeatedly challenged me to say "yes" when I most felt like saying "no."

Bourgeault, C. *Love Is Stronger than Death, Mystical Hope, The Wisdom Way of Knowing, The Heart of Centering Prayer*. These books accompanied and continue to accompany me through my daring adventure, each appearing at just the right time to deepen both my understanding and my experience of choosing heaven on earth. In *Love Is Stronger than Death* I found a map that inspired me at each step of my adventure. *Mystical Hope* opened my heart to an enduring hope that allowed me to see beyond my expectations. *The Wisdom Way of Knowing* offered tools for navigating the twists and turns of my journey, and *The Heart of Centering Prayer* brought me the deeper understanding necessary for continuing to choose heaven on earth when it seemed least accessible.

Frankel, E. *The wisdom of not knowing: Discovering a life of wonder by embracing uncertainty.* In the introduction to this book the author states the following: "In Jewish mysticism, divinity is the ultimate *unknown* and *unknowable* reality that, paradoxically, we are enjoined to know." Choosing heaven on earth is, I believe, the first step in coming to know that unknowable reality. As such, it involves just what the title of this book expresses: "discovering a life of wonder by embracing uncertainty." I found reading it to of immeasurable help in doing so.

DEEPENING LOVE, HOPE, AND FAITH

As [the diver] drops deeper and deeper into the abyss,
slowly his eyes begin to pick up the luminous
quality of the darkness; what was fear is relaxed and
he moves into the lower region with
confidence and peculiar vision
(H. Thurman)

I'd thought I knew what it was to love, hope and faith[38] as I started my adventure. I was proven wrong on all three counts, frustratingly so at times and delightfully so at others. My love, hope and faith were repeatedly challenged as my adventure took me into territory that refused to conform to the maps I'd set out to chart its course. The second key to sustaining heaven on earth—*deepening love, hope and faith*—began to be forged as I realized the degree to which fear diminished my ability to love, discouragement threatened my hope and undesired or unanticipated external conditions weakened my faith.

The words of a 20th century African American mystic provided me with an apt image for my experience: "en route to the floor of the ocean the diver first passes through the 'belt of the fishes.' This is a wide band of light reflected from the surface of the sea. From this area he moves to a depth of water that cannot be penetrated by light above the surface. It is dark, for[e]boding, and eerie. The diver's immediate reaction is apt to be one of fear and sometimes a sudden spasm of panic..."

If one can find the courage to go deeper, however, everything changes: "As he [the diver] drops deeper and deeper into the abyss, slowly his eyes begin to pick up the luminous quality of the darkness; what was fear is relaxed and he moves into the lower region with confidence and peculiar vision."[39] This second key was forged as I found myself dropping deeper and deeper into my understanding and experience of love, hope and faith.

DEEPENING LOVE

At first, I could not see beyond all that defined love for me (e.g., my beloved friend's presence and his repeated affirmations of love through frequent calls and letters). When these markers began to lessen, it seemed to be only a process of deepening loss. It took time, frustration and steadfast commitment to shift my focus from what I believed I was leaving behind to what I was being offered. As I did, I began to see that the changes I feared did not signal loss. Instead, they signaled a process of deepening gift. Gradually, an edge-less mystery unfolded, embracing me with a love beyond any of the conditions and illusions to which I'd imagined it must adhere.

My love deepened in ways unimagined and unanticipated each time I chose to say "Yes!" to its presence when its form was not as I wished. Each "Yes!" awakened a deeper love, part and parcel of an Infinite Light and Love yet also somehow still me. Stripped of conditions and illusions, love showed its truest face: a soul energy revealing Infinite Light and Love "while at the same time making it available as a fragrance and nutrient."[40]

Deepening Hope

As my love deepened, my hope also began to be transformed. Sharon Salzberg makes a distinction between deep hope and "fixated" hope; i.e., hope dependent on external conditions and expectation. The latter, Salzberg asserts, is "one of the most subtle ways fear can bind us, so quietly we hardly know to call it fear."[41]

As I read those words I awakened to the lack of depth in my own hope. When all was good in the world around me (according to me), particularly in my relationship with my beloved friend, my hope was strong. When all was not good, however, I'd become increasingly frustrated and my hope weakened. I'd fixate my hope all the more then, much like someone adding more glue to a picture that keeps falling off the wall,.

Releasing the conditions I'd believed must be present to keep hope alive, like releasing the conditions I'd placed on love, seemed only loss at first. Slowly, as I cycled between hopelessness and hopefulness, my hope began to deepen. The reality against which I stumbled carved pathways that turned hope into something whose substance supported and strengthened rather than merely promised. Its reality as gift rather than loss emerged as I found the courage to hope without the need to expect or impose desired outcomes.

Gradually, my focus shifted from hope tied to the realization of my expectations to hope as an "abiding state of being."[42] While love opened the door to sustaining heaven on earth, it was deep hope as an abiding state of being that kept it open.

Deepening Faith

The discontinuity between what was and what was not yet brought with it the realization of my faith's fragility. As times when all went well alternated with times when nothing seemed to be right, it was difficult to continue to have faith in the rightness of my journey. Almost imperceptibly, faith's assurance that all was well would become increasingly imprisoned within walls of fear that strangled my ability to trust in an undefined future. I couldn't believe that outside the limitations imposed by my fear was a vast reality beyond anything I could conceive, waiting to unfold. Yet, it was there, outside those limitations, that my faith deepened.

There, faith allowed me to embrace and enter into my doubt to seek out its music in the seemingly silent and empty spaces between notes. There, beyond mental convictions and rote beliefs, faith became something I lived rather than possessed. Though questions did not cease to haunt and disturb me, I learned that if I held the doubt in my heart without trying to resolve it with my mind, I created a womb within which unimagined answers were birthed. I faithed, just as I loved and hoped.

THREE MOVEMENTS

Over time I realized that below the specific mechanics of the situations whose challenges deepened my love, hope and faith were three common movements. The first was a shift from a focus on the forms I believed defined love, hope and faith (i.e., external expressions and conditions) to a focus on their essence, which lay below and beyond any form.

As I was drawn ever more intensely along the path carved by friendship, I discovered the love that remained, buried deep beneath my fear of its loss. The conditions I'd always placed around love were revealed to be only external clothing hiding its deeper essence. Similarly, freed from external expectations, the essence of my hope emerged. A deeper hope blossomed to reveal Infinite Love and Light beyond any I'd imagined, even in darkness. At the same time, the faith that gradually surfaced as my love and hope deepened and stabilized, led me into its essence: trust rooted in increasing intimacy with Infinite Love and Light.

The second movement involved diving into the mystery that lay below and beyond the limitations of the faculties that gave form to my love, hope and faith: logic, mental reasoning, will, and memory. Richard Rohr gives a definition of mystery that is particularly applicable. He defines mystery not as something that cannot be known but as something that is infinitely knowable.[43] While finite knowing can define external forms, it cannot hold the mystery of infinite knowability.

As another modern day mystic puts it, "I can't put the ocean into a thimble, but I can drop the thimble into the ocean."[44] The second movement involved just that: putting the finite "thimble" of what I believed and wanted love, hope and faith to be into the oceanic mystery of their infinite knowability.

Opening my heart to that infinite knowability, which I could neither comprehend nor hold with my logic, mental reasoning, will or memory, became the third movement that completed the forging of the second key to sustaining heaven on earth. When I released form and dived into the wider expanse of the formless mystery at the heart of love, hope and faith, I discovered that only such opening can be truly responsive to heaven on earth. Only the heart can hold what the mind cannot. Only in the heart can love, hope and faith become "deeply embodied as a vibration, a homing frequency to which we can become increasingly sensitively attuned."[45] With an open heart knowing becomes not a taking or getting but a "participation in a living relational field" where heaven on earth is "simultaneously intimate and cosmic."[46]

As I cycled from form to mystery to opening, my love

deepened, drawing me ever more intensely along the path carved by friendship, both human and divine. A deeper hope blossomed, revealing the face of Infinite Love and Light present even in darkness and, simultaneously, a deeper faith brought me into increasing intimacy with that face.

Scripture Reflection

*You are like a smart carpenter who built his
house on solid rock. Rain poured down, the
river flooded, a tornado hit—but nothing
moved that house. It was fixed to the rock.*
(Matthew 7: 24-25, *The Message*)

As before, I turned once again to scripture to seek resonance
for my experience of deepening love, hope and faith, the rock
to which I was learning to fix my spiritual house. I found that
resonance in Jesus' repeated questions to Peter (John 21:15). As
this second key was being forged, I heard those questions once
again as if spoken to me:

"Do you love me?"

"Do you love me?"

"Do you love me?"

This time I heard their underlying challenges:

"Do you love me with a love deep enough to release the
conditions you've imposed on it and go beyond what you believe
defines it?"

"Do you love me with hope deep enough to sustain your
commitment to heaven on earth when your expectations are not
fulfilled?"

"Do you love me with deep enough faith to keep believing
when all evidence for heaven on earth seems to have disappeared?"

I realized all three were asking the same thing: "Are you
willing to allow yourself to sink into the reality that lies below
and beyond the absence of all you've thought defined love, hope
and faith and there wait until the luminosity of their essence sheds
light and rises to fill their form once more?" It was a question that
touched on a reality I was only beginning to believe could be.

I said yes, as I had before, though perhaps a little less

confidently. My yes now was tinged by a greater awareness that I was affirming not only what already was. I was also affirming the yet unknown still to come. I could only stop and wait in darkness, remembering that light emerges almost imperceptibly as night slowly transforms into dawn.

Selected Practices to Support Deepening Love, Hope, and Faith

Initially, the deepening of my love, hope and faith was primarily promoted spontaneously by the joy and challenges of my daring adventure with my beloved friend. I did not set out to intentionally deepen my love, hope or faith. I simply focused on figuring out how to respond to specific situations in ways that would not result in the loss of the wondrous love offered me by my beloved friend or of the heaven on earth it awakened in me. My focus shifted and became more intentional only as situations that did not conform to my (or at times his) expectations challenged my love, hope and faith. It shifted further still in response to his physical absence after his passing.

A primary practice on which I came to rely as this shift happened is a deceptively simple one grounded in a phrase borrowed from the title of a book by Peter Block: *The Answer to How Is Yes*. I discovered that saying yes to the presence of heaven on earth in my life however disguised it might be by the narratives my thoughts, beliefs and fear attached to it, always in and of itself, deepened my love, hope and faith. It expressed my commitment even if I did not yet know how I would live it out or where it would take me.

Another writer has talked about both the risk and promise of saying yes:

"… say Yes, again and again and again.
And Yes some more. Let us pray dangerously,
The most dangerous prayer is *Yes*."[47]

It was from this perspective that I began the practice of saying yes as a support to the deepening of my love, hope and faith.

A second more spiritually framed practice became

39

complementary to my practice of saying yes. Traditionally called "putting the mind in the heart,"[48] this practice clarified that to which I was saying yes. Cynthia Bourgeault quotes a defining aspect of this practice from *The Cloud of Unknowing*: "God may be reached and held close by means of love, but by means of thought never."[49]

Putting the mind in the heart prioritizes relational insight (i.e., heart-sight) over conceptual reasoning (i.e., mind-sight). For me, it meant filtering my rational thoughts and perceptions through the lens of my heart's more intuitive knowing. I found two questions helpful in doing this: Am I choosing to believe what my mind and its fears tell me is true about this situation or circumstance? Am I willing to believe what my heart's intuition and insight know to be true over that my mind tells me is true? Answering yes to the first always cast heaven on earth into doubt. Answering yes to the second always brought it firmly to the forefront and sustained it there.

While I could consciously and intentionally will to choose heaven on earth, deepening my love, hope and faith was not an act of will. I could only practice saying Yes and putting my mind in my heart.

Book Providence

As always, books that affirmed and supported my path and the forging of this second key appeared as if by magic, found in bookstores, on the internet, or suggested by friends. Here are some. The first three focus specifically on love, hope and faith. The others speak to these more indirectly, sometimes without even mentioning the words yet still addressing their presence.

Nouwen, H. *The inner voice of love: A journey from anguish to love*. In this book Nouwen presents what he calls "spiritual imperatives" to aid in learning to recognize and accept love. I found many of these imperatives deeply helpful as I navigated my own journey to recognize and accept my beloved friend's love.

Lamott, A. *Almost everything: Notes on hope*. I found this book both delightful and enlightening. It weaves an intricate yet ever truthful path between the aspects of our daily reality that inspire hope and those that seem to deny that very hope.

Salzberg, S. *Faith: Trusting your own deepest experience*. This book introduced me to the contrast between abiding hope and fixated hope. As it drew my attention to trusting my "own deepest experience" it helped to deepen my faith as well as my hope and love.

Block, P. *The answer to how is yes*. Though not explicitly a book on spirituality, this book gave me practical tools for putting my mind, which always sought HOW, in my heart that I might say "yes." Its multiple concrete examples helped me to better discern the difference between the two.

Ryan, S. *Praying dangerously, Radical reliance on God*. The insights I found in this book both expanded and affirmed my practice of saying yes in the absence of a HOW. In reading it I was repeatedly reminded that saying yes again and again was relevant not only to choosing heaven on earth but also to deepening my love, hope and faith.

SEEING WITH BINOCULAR VISION

*Thou hast in thy soul **two eyes**, which are*
set together back to back; the one looketh into
[heaven], the other looketh into nature.
(J. Boehme)

A metaphor used by Jacob Boehme inspired my name for this key. Boehme, a 17ᵗʰ century mystic, believed that just as we have two physical eyes we also have two spiritual eyes that see distinct yet not contradictory images. One eye looks out at earth's sensory physical world. The other's gaze is fixed on heaven, the non-physical realm within and beyond that world. When the images of each eye, like the images from our physical eyes, are aligned and integrated, they join into one: heaven on earth. According to Richard Rohr such vision—binocular vision—allows a "second gaze" through which we see something in its particularity yet also in a much larger frame.[50]

As I reflected on binocular vision, I realized that it is about more than merely seeing and connecting two images. There is a difference between seeing heaven *and* earth and seeing heaven *on* earth. For most of my life I'd believed that if I could see heaven *and* earth, I could then also see heaven *on* earth. Only now did I begin to realize that what I had actually been doing was laying two images—heaven and earth—side by side, putting them together yet keeping them separate. After all, one was not at all like the other.

I learned to truly see heaven *on* earth only as I struggled with the contradictions I perceived between my desired experience of friendship (i.e., heaven) and my actual experience (i.e., earth). My inability to integrate the two not only diminished and at times totally erased my ability to delight in the joy and wonder of my connection with my beloved friend, it also diminished and at times totally erased my ability to sustain heaven on earth.

While I did not fully realize it at the time, my image of heaven and earth was largely monocular, composed of two smaller images that remained separate. I tended to think of earth (ordinary life) "here" and heaven (the joy and light I experienced) somewhere "there," coming from and largely dependent on external circumstances. In a sense, I could see heaven with one eye and earth with the other but could not fuse the two into one binocular image that integrated them without erasing their distinctions. Even as I saw both sides of this duality I remained unaware that the distinctions themselves were rooted in duality and inevitably led me to making a choice of half over whole.[51]

It wasn't that I was unaware of non-duality. My *understanding* of non-duality, the key to binocular seeing, started to form some years before my adventure challenged me to translate it into the *experience* of binocular vision vis-à-vis heaven on earth. It was an understanding developed within an academic context in which I addressed respectful, reciprocal and responsive communication across culturally diverse environments.[52] In that context I had even developed the concept of what I called 3rd Space, an interactional space that encompasses and integrates diverse cultural and other perspectives. Yet, both my understanding of non-duality and of 3rd Space remained separate from my spiritual journey until my adventure of love. Without realizing it, I'd ironically encased them in my own unexamined duality of secular-professional and spiritual-personal.

That duality did not finally resolve until I faced the challenge of the contradictions that cast shadows on my adventure with my beloved friend. It was in the face of that challenge that I finally expanded my non-dual 3rd Space perspective to include my experiences with my beloved friend and discovered seeing with binocular vision as key to sustaining heaven on earth.

With binocular vision, I no longer needed to make a choice of heaven over earth—or vice versa. Seeing both at the same time no longer meant blurring their differences or needing to prefer one over the other. When all seemed perfect (i.e., "heaven"), I no longer felt I needed to keep all that was less than perfect (i.e., "earth") at arm's length, fearing that it would somehow diminish that perfection. Vice versa, when all seemed imperfect and flawed, I did not need to believe that heaven was absent, somewhere other than where I was. The following words from my earlier book mark the beginning emergence of this shift into seeing heaven on earth with binocular vision: "To separate heaven (i.e., love, beauty, awe, wonder) from earth's trials is 'to lose the personal intimacy' of God's infinite self playing through the chords of my being. To separate earth's trials from heaven is 'to lose the cosmic vastness' of Infinite Light and Love within which their sting can be softened."[53]

Two aspects of binocular vision are particularly significant to its function as a key to sustaining heaven on earth. The first of these is its <u>relational</u> nature. Binocular vision does not see the world with sharply defined parts separate from each other. Instead, it reveals a world where each "separate" piece is deeply, albeit paradoxically, entangled with every other. From this relational perspective binocular vision makes it possible to perceive seemingly contradictory realities as simultaneously distinct and equally present.

Three particular contradictions that regularly challenged my ability to sustain heaven on earth concretized this non-polarizing aspect of binocular vision for me in relation to heaven on earth. The first, and for a long time the most troublesome one, was the contradiction between presence and absence: the presence and absence of my beloved friend as well as the presence and absence of my felt experience of heaven on earth. A second and related contradiction was the contradiction between knowing and unknowing. Not knowing (i.e., understanding) what was happening or when something would happen triggered fear or confusion and shook my certainty of heaven on earth. The third and, I later realized, most central contradiction was the contradiction between holding on and letting go. It was this contradiction that was at the root of my struggles with presence and absence as well as with knowing and unknowing. I wanted to hold on to presence in the face of absence and I resisted letting go of what I knew. [54]

Presence and absence. With binocular vision I started to recognize that absence no longer erased presence. I came to see that both were in fact necessary and complementary. My sense of my beloved friend's presence was no longer something irreconcilable with his absence. In fact I discovered that it was only my keeping them apart that erased one when the other was there.

I stated my early understanding of this discovery in my previous book with the following words: "Without presence, absence becomes only emptiness, devoid of life and love…. Without absence, presence loses its capacity for intimacy and becomes only what we can possess and control."[55]

<u>Knowing and unknowing</u>. The contradiction I'd always found between knowing and unknowing was similarly dissolved with binocular vision. Rather than an obstacle to knowing, seeing with binocular vision allowed not knowing (i.e., unknowing) to become the doorway into the intimacy of a deeper knowing that lay just beyond the strictures of my certainty. With binocular vision I could focus on getting to know my experiences as they were rather than as I believed them to be based on my established knowing. I no longer needed to squeeze heaven on earth into what I already knew. I could allow it to stretch beyond my knowing.

<u>Holding on and letting go</u>. Binocular vision also allowed me to see through the apparent contradiction between holding on and letting go. Much too often this contradiction had meant "losing" heaven as I tried to hold on to earth, or vice versa, missing what was right in front of me, "on earth" as I clung to my experience of heaven. As I began to develop binocular vision, however, I discovered that letting go of my efforts to keep them apart, which initially felt like not caring, did the opposite. Holding on to one dimmed rather than safeguarded the other as I'd intended. With binocular vision, I began to realize that I did not need to choose between these realities, or between any others that appeared contradictory to me. I could instead hold both simultaneously, allowing their reconciliation and integration to evolve on its own.

The second significant aspect of binocular vision as key to living heaven on earth is the <u>perceptual shift</u> it engenders. Though seeing with binocular vision did not change what I saw, it did change *how* I saw. In doing so, it allowed me to define what I saw in entirely new ways. Rather than merely taking things for they seemed on the surface (e.g., he hasn't called, he must no longer want to talk with me), binocular vision allowed me to put them into a deeper context that often flipped their meaning (e.g., he's actually tried to call several times but has been interrupted by other calls, which I later discovered was actually what happened). My focus shifted from the external surface of things, which distinguished them, to their underlying essence, which united them. I learned to ask myself "This is only what one eye is seeing, what might the whole picture be if I joined it with the other eye?).

Both the relational and perception-shifting aspects of binocular vision come together to shape its third aspect: its nature as a portal (i.e., key) to experiencing heaven *on* earth. Binocular vision transformed "nucleated" understandings of earth as object separate from heaven into perceptions of it as a "flowing, unboundaried" sphere that is, in the words of Julian of Norwich, "oned" with heaven.[56]

"Oneing" distinct forms in this way may not be typical, yet it is neither esoteric nor difficult. I had in fact already been doing so daily without being aware of it. When I looked at a picture, for example, I didn't think "Oh, this part is foreground, which contradicts the background. I can't look at both at the same time." Instead, I saw foreground and background "oned" into a whole image while still retaining my ability to identify background as background and foreground as foreground. The challenge that binocular vision posed for me in relation to heaven on earth was not in developing a new ability. It was rather in giving up my certainty that certain things could only be, or mean, this one thing and, consequently, that the very existence of another contrasting thing was somehow threatened.

Thankfully, the role of binocular vision as a key to opening our perception of the world as "oned," is once again being increasingly recognized in Western cultures.[57] That broader recognition helped me greatly as I began to develop binocular vision.

SCRIPTURAL REFLECTION

*...look at the birds. Walk out into the
fields and look at the wildflowers.*
(Matthew 6: 26,27, The Message)

As I turned to scripture yet again, I realized the degree to which Jesus pointed to earth's realities when asked about heaven, He repeatedly recognized and pointed to the voice and presence of Infinite Light and Love (i.e., heaven) in people, flowers, and birds, even in the very ground itself. I had always known this yet it was only as I gained binocular vision that I began to more fully realize the degree to which earth, with all its limitations and flaws, is both mirror and part of heaven's reality. As I thought about that now I began to wonder:

How might I have understood your words about creation had I been there to hear them myself? I know that though I mostly did not think of heaven and earth as contradictory realities, I tended to keep them in relatively separate compartments. I did not often think of heaven as I looked at what was around me. In fact, I often thought of its absence, especially as I saw things that contradicted my ideas of how it should be.

It was not until my own adventure of love challenged me to experience both heaven and earth as simultaneously present that my thinking began to change. Only then did I begin to consciously and intentionally seek to perceive and sustain their integration.

Perhaps that integration was what you wanted me to realize. Perhaps you wanted me to see and experience heaven through earth's realities with greater awareness, especially when earth seemed far from "heavenly."

I hear your words once more, both spoken and unspoken:
"Look at the birds. Walk out into the fields and look at

the wildflowers." They are not perfect. Neither are they always beautiful. Yet they are always mirror and part of heaven.

"Love your neighbor." Your neighbor may seldom be perfect. Your neighbor may not be beautiful. Yet, your neighbor too is always mirror and part of heaven.

I hear your message so much more clearly now: See not heaven and earth as you look at birds, fields, wildflowers and neighbors. See heaven <u>on</u> earth. I think that's what I might have heard had I spent time with you as you walked on earth. At least it is what I hear now.

Selected Practices to Support Binocular Vision

Binocular vision acknowledges the distinctive differences of existing realities (e.g., absence, presence; heaven, earth) while simultaneously acknowledging (or at least allowing us to imagine) their indivisibility. The primary challenge of binocular vision is giving up the certainty that things that are different are thereby also contradictory and must be kept apart if one is not to somehow diminish the other. Interestingly, while I had become familiar with binocular vision in an academic setting and had even written about it,[58] it took me much longer to adopt conscious practices to support it in relation to my relationship with my beloved friend as well as to sustaining heaven on earth. Two particularly helpful practices I adopted were reframing and Byron Katie's "The Work."

Reframing. Behind reframing is the premise that "many of the circumstances that seem …[contradictory]…may only appear so based on a framework of assumptions we carry with us. Draw a different frame around the same set of circumstances [i.e., re-frame them] and new pathways come into view."[59] The practice of reframing in relation to sustaining heaven on earth involved examining the framework of assumptions behind my perception of a particular situation as contradictory to another and then asking why I perceived it to be so under these circumstances but not those (e.g., why I perceived my friend to be absent some times and not others, for example).

Reframing in this way helped me to remove the blockages that contradictions so often posed to my experience of heaven on earth. I learned to take two things I perceived as contradictory (e.g., he loved me yet hadn't called me in several weeks) and brainstorm how they might in fact be complementary. How might

I, for example, perceive my friend's not calling as complementary to his loving me rather than as a contradiction of it? When, for example, I reframed my friend's not calling as a reflection of his trust that our love could allow him to do what he needed to do, his not calling became an affirmation of heaven on earth rather than a denial of it.

I found a degree of playfulness and creativity useful in practicing reframing. Two nonsensical examples demonstrate how such playfulness and creativity can bring non-similar things together: "What happens when you cross a checkerboard with a midnight snack? You get edible crackers with the motto 'Beat them and eat them.' What if you cross high-heeled shoes with a tricycle? You get shoes with training wheels."[60]

Reframing is a practice that cannot be easily summarized or laid out in sequential steps. It involves a creative right-brain process that is neither logical nor linear. For that reason the books I found most helpful were books that illustrated its use rather than those that gave detailed instruction (e.g., *Yiddishe Kop: Creative problem solving in Jewish learning, lore and humor*).

The Work. A second practice that supported my development of binocular vision comes from Byron Katie's "The Work."[61] Like reframing, this technique is one intended to take us out of the certainty with which we cling to our narratives about specific events and circumstances (e.g., this didn't happen and that means X; if this happens, that will mean Y).

The four questions Katie describes in her book *Loving what is: Four questions that can change your life* were especially helpful to me in developing binocular vision. Though binocular vision is not addressed in the design or description of these questions, they support its development in that they stimulate cognitive flexibility in perceiving and understanding specific situations or problems.

Each question is in some way intended to help us release our certainty of their meaning. The first two questions are quite straightforward: "Is it true? Can you absolutely know it's true?" These questions focused me on the nature of just what it was that I was finding problematic The point was not to ascertain its truth but rather to reflect more mindfully on the degree to which I believed it. [62]

The third question deepened that reflection: "How do you react, what happens, when you believe that thought?" Katie recommends that no judgment be attached to the answer or, if it is, that that judgment be set aside for subsequent inquiry. This third question shifted my attention from what I believed to my relationship with that belief. It focused me on myself as creator of that belief rather than as an external observer of a fixed reality. I found myself asking how do I react, what happens, when I believe that my experience of heaven on earth is no longer present or real?" For me this question opened the door to another. It was a question implied silently as I considered the one asked explicitly: "Do I have a choice to believe and/or react differently?"

The fourth and final question Katie poses is "Who would you be without that thought?" That question fully pushed open the door to the one I heard silently. I wanted to have a choice because I knew that without the thought that I was finding X problematic I'd once again be someone able to experience heaven on earth no matter the circumstances.

BOOK PROVIDENCE

As this key was being forged, sources on non-dual and paradoxical perception kept coming to my attention. While some were distinctly spiritual, most were more focused on the area of business and leadership. (I can't help but wonder what this says about the degree of attention paid to diversity of viewpoints and playfulness in spiritual writings!)

Bourgeault, C. *The heart of centering prayer: Nondual Christianity in theory and practice.* Cynthia's writings in this book on unitive vision and the heart as an organ of perception provided me with a solid spiritual understanding of binocular vision along with some general steps for developing it.

Bonder, M. *Yiddishe Kop: Creative problem solving in Jewish learning, lore and humor.* This is a delightful and at times frustrating book that explores transcending the limits of what our mind and reason insist is the only possible way to see and interpret life's sacred dimensions. The use of reframing is evident in many of the examples Bonder uses as he describes four realms of reality: the apparent realm of the apparent, the hidden realm of the apparent, the apparent realm of the hidden, and the hidden realm of the hidden.

Taylor, B. B. *An altar in the world: A geography of faith.* This book is all about discovering the sacred is all around us. Though binocular seeing is never mentioned, it is definitely modeled in the integration of spiritual "invisible" reality with external and very visible reality.

Newell, J. P. *The book of creation: An introduction to Celtic spirituality.* This book, like Taylor's book, exemplifies binocular vision. The author connects spiritual reality and concrete reality through each "day" of creation.

I found more explicit steps to developing binocular vision in other "non-spiritual" books such as the following:.

Katie, B. *Loving what is: Four questions that can change your life.* This book provided me with the four questions I used in my practice as well as with many fun exercises for learning how to see the complementarity of things I typically perceived as contradictory.

Fletcher, J. & Olwyler, K. *Paradoxical thinking: How to profit from your contradictions.* This book is one of very few I found that contains very specific steps for reframing contradictions. It provides a rich complement to Katie's book from a more general perspective.

Dobson, T. and Miller, V. *Aikido in everyday life.* This book applies the principles of Aikido, a non-violent martial art, to interpersonal situations. It provides concrete exercises for choosing how to respond to conflicts and dissonances in ways that promote harmony, using shapes to illustrate them.

Martin, R. *The opposable mind: How successful leaders win through integrative thinking.* This book is a celebration of what the author calls an "opposable mind," which I would call a mind with the capacity for binocular vision. In the author's words: "we are born with an opposable mind we can use to hold two conflicting ideas in constructive tension." Though focused on secular business leaders, this book provided me with many concrete ideas on using binocular vision from a spiritual perspective.

Perkins, D. *The eureka effect: The art and logic of breakthrough thinking.* This book offers insights into unimagined options and shifts in perception that reveal new paths to desired goals.

Zander, R. S. and Zander, B. *The art of possibility: Transforming professional and personal life.* Zander and Zander describe this book as "a how-to book of an unusual kind" and it is just that. Its content contains multiple examples of binocular seeing.

READING LIFE AS SACRED TEXT

The cosmos is like a living sacred text that
we can learn to read and interpret.
(J.P. Newell)

The forging of this fourth key—Reading Life as Sacred Text—was marked by a subtle yet unmistakable shift in how I found myself framing sustaining heaven on earth. I'd initially framed it within the challenges posed by the concrete and very earthly dimensions of my friendship with my beloved friend. When those concrete earthly dimensions were lost with my friend's passing, I found myself facing an irrevocably changed heaven on earth where neither heaven nor earth were any longer as they had been. My challenge then became discerning heaven on earth without my friend's physical presence, which had so concretely and wondrously affirmed it.

Surprisingly, I began to discover that the union of heaven on earth deepened rather than lessened as I'd feared. I found a heaven now made more personal and vivid with the inclusion of my friend's presence[63] and an earth now both hollowed and hallowed. While the writings of both Christian (e.g., St. John of the Cross, St. Teresa of Avila) and non-Christian (e.g., Rumi, Llewellyn Vaughn-Lee) mystics affirm such a heaven on earth beyond the physical manifestations of earth's realities, I had not yet truly known it.

Two questions posed by Tosha Silver in her book *Outrageous openness: Letting the divine take the lead* crystallized my newfound understanding: "…what if we each have this [Divine] ardent inner suitor who's writing us love letters every day …?" What if [Infinite Light and Love] is constantly igniting roadside flares to get our attention? [64] I began to realize that I could continue to sustain the heaven on earth I'd found with my friend if I used these questions in place of my friend's physical presence to discern heaven on earth happening for me and with me (i.e., to read my life as sacred text.

After reading and reflecting on the perspective highlighted by Silver's questions, I realized I had already been doing so, except in reverse! I had been reading my life as text that spoke of the separation of heaven on earth rather than of their union. It had always been easy, almost reflexive, for me to read my life for places where I believed heaven on earth was somehow missing and then look for ways to remedy that. When I didn't hear from my friend, for example, or when a planned reunion did not come about, my first response was almost always to take it as a sign of heaven no longer on earth and then seek ways of re-connecting with it once more. That focus, in fact, provided a major impetus for the forging of the first three keys.

At the beginning of our relationship, my friend would always reassure me when I feared all would be lost and could no longer sustain heaven on earth. With his reassurance, all would once again be OK. His words were, in fact, love letters. It was the loss of these love letters after his passing that stimulated a shift into a different perspective on reading my life and began the forging of this fourth key.

Rather than focusing on sustaining heaven on earth, as do the earlier keys, Reading Life as Sacred Text focuses on living the certainty of a heaven on earth already sustained. It searches for love letters, the "manifestation of [the] universal truth [that] matter [i.e., earth] is, and always has been, the hiding place for Spirit [i.e., heaven], forever offering itself to be discovered [and read]."[65] With this key I began to see my life experiences and circumstances as love letters as well as, at times, roadside flares alerting me to my loss of alignment with heaven and earth.

The perception of an ever-present infinite and uncreated light and love underlying and permeating finite reality (i.e., heaven on earth) is an ancient one reflected in Celtic spirituality.[66] The writings of Eriugena and Pelagius, for example, are characterized by the belief that heaven exists comprehensively on earth: "in all people, in all places, [in all circumstances], in all created thing," even when "buried and forgotten under layers of" misperception and darkness. [67] At those latter times, when heaven on earth seems only a fairytale, Reading Life as Sacred Text provided me with a key for sustaining heaven on earth by unearthing what remained true: the fact that "the whole world is conspiring to shower [us] with blessings."[68]

At its core, Reading Life as Sacred Text celebrates incarnation: non-physical reality (i.e., Infinite Light and Love) in intimate communion with physical reality, each unique yet also one with the other. It is guided by a single question: "How is heaven on earth engaging with me at this time through this experience?"

Four elements helped shape my answer to that question: trust, reciprocity, inclusivity, and the act of reading itself. Trust is essential to interpreting what is being communicated in any relationship whether human to human or human to divine. Trust does not, however, come full-blown; it must be developed. Richard Rohr's three-step description of spiritual development can also be applied to the development of trust: order, disorder, re-order. That is the pattern the development of my own trust followed, both in relation to my beloved friend and in relation to reading my life as sacred text.

At the beginning, my trust in my friend's love seemed full-blown, the product of my decision to connect with him and with a heaven on earth beyond any I'd imagined. After a time, though, it began to unravel in the face of experiences that undermined my confidence (e.g., when my friend acted in ways I could not understand). Could I trust in his continuing love when he didn't call for several weeks? Trust in the sacred text of my life (i.e, heaven on earth concretely present in my life) frayed in a similar fashion when I could see no answer to my prayers and my confidence in heaven on earth eroded.

Over time I realized that this fraying of my trust was in fact a necessary prelude to learning to read my life as sacred text in the absence of my friend's physical presence. It revealed the limits of the ordinary everyday lenses through which I saw and interpreted the events and circumstance of my life. Through those lenses, I too easily missed the sacred dimensions of my life that lay beyond.

The first three keys to sustaining heaven on earth—Choosing Heaven on Earth, Deepening Love, Hope and Faith, and Seeing with Binocular Vision—gave me new lenses. They brought forth the sacred dimensions embedded in my life's text like invisible ink exposed to heat. My trust re-ordered as I used those keys, allowing me to open radically to Infinite Light and Love (i.e., heaven) incarnate and incarnating in the concrete events and circumstances of my life.

Sacred text is not text that is only sacred. It is text that is also and simultaneously just text. The second element that supported reading my life as sacred text was reciprocity. For a long time, I failed to realize I was missing that reciprocity, which I've come to realize is a critical element in all deep relationships, be they fully in the human realm or across human and divine realms.

Much as there must be reciprocity between lover and beloved in a human relationship, so too must there be reciprocity between finite reality and infinite reality. It is a paradoxical reciprocity to be sure. It neither means nor requires that there be equal power or status, only that infinite (i.e., the sacred dimension of those events and circumstances) and finite (i.e., life's concrete events and circumstances) be allowed equal voice (i.e., presence).

Missing reciprocity, I privileged heaven (wasn't it more powerful and perfect?) even as I paid more attention to earth (it was so much more immediate and concrete). The first (i.e., heaven) brought me inspiration but the second (i.e., earth) put brakes on that inspiration. After all, what if the inspiration took me out of my comfort zone (which ironically it often did)? Gradually though, reciprocity began to transform the tension between the two. I learned what one mystic in particular has explicitly recognized: the paradox that lies at the heart of reciprocity: "True union ... differentiates the elements it brings together."[69]

A third element essential to my reading of my life as sacred text was inclusivity. Reading my life as sacred text needed to be inclusive of all parts of my life not just the "heaven" parts I deemed sacred. Heaven's reality emerges *on earth*, within earth's flaws and imperfections. That is, in fact, the only way it can do so.[70] To paraphrase Rilke: Perhaps what most disturbs us—what we find most difficult to accept—is only an aspect of heaven on earth waiting to be set free from earth's limitations and our own misperceptions and illusions, which hold it captive.[71]

I learned to accept my friend's actions as part of heaven on earth when they were other than I wanted or liked only after repeatedly finding out that their meaning was other than I insisted it must be. When I began to accept them without judging them through my own misperceptions and illusions I truly began to read them as being as much a part of my life's sacred text as the other aspects that were more in line with what I wanted or liked. Amazingly, I continue to learn this wider inclusivity even after my friend's passing. The lens of my misperceptions and illusions continues to soften now that there is no longer a human relationship to protect or defend.[72]

The fourth element I discovered essential to reading the text of my life as sacred was the act of reading itself. One of the Merriam-Webster dictionary definitions of reading is the following: "to study the movements of with mental formulation of the communication expressed." Silver's dichotomy of love letters and roadside flares provided me with a simple though not always easy mental formulation for reading life as sacred text.[73]

Identifying and sorting events and circumstances of my life (i.e., the text) into roadside flares and love letters was not always a straightforward task. Love was not always expressed in ways I believed it should be (by either me or my friend). Love letters did not always seem to be love letters at all. Roadside flares often seemed to be signs of things not going well rather than signals reminding me to look at the road more carefully; i.e., to read my life at a deeper level.

After my friend's passing I developed some guiding questions to better guide my reading: Is this event or circumstance a roadside flare alerting me to the fact that I'm paying attention to something to which I need to stop paying attention? Is it calling to stop and wait before I move on? Is this event or circumstance a love letter from the Divine? Have I opened it or am I leaving it unopened? Am I receiving it with an open heart, without taking or clinging and without any sense of obligation to reciprocate? Have I said thanks?

Answers to these questions came easily or quickly at times, revealed in what were clearly love letters from heaven on earth (e.g., my certain sense of continued connection with my beloved friend in spirit). At other times, they came much less quickly or easily, disguised as roadside flares (e.g., the loss of my sense of connection with my friend in spirit). Getting to the best answers involved not only using all previous elements, it often also involved returning to earlier keys. At times, like waiting for a rose to bloom, it was necessary to simply remain open and "live the questions,"[74] much like Zen koans.[75] When this was the case, it became not so much about finding answers as about opening to the dimensions or realms of reality that lay "hidden," outside of what was comprehensible through my reason and logic.[76]

Over time I realized just how deeply Reading Life as Sacred Text is grounded in the heart rather than the mind. It offers its "answers" primarily from and through lived relationship rather than objective analysis.

Scripture Reflection

Look at the birds free and unfettered, …careless
in the care of God. …look at the wildflowers.
They neither primp or shop, but have you
ever seen color or design quite like it?
(Matthew 6:25-28, The Message)

Reading life as sacred text is rooted in a dialogue between human and divine that allows for the reception of heaven on earth as well as for its expression in return. I turned once again to find resonance of this in scripture. I imagined walking beside Jesus as I had often done in the past, listening to him talk about the beauty of the wildflowers along the road and the songs of the birds that nested in the trees above us:

You'd called my attention to heaven's reflection in nature before. This time, though, I sensed that you wanted me to pay attention in a different way. This time, as you talked about them, I became aware that you did not see or hear them as objects apart from you. This time I understood that for you they were not just "out there." Their beauty and song did not just reflect heaven on earth. They were actually within and part of heaven on earth in the same way as we were. They brought heaven on earth into concrete form perceivable by our human senses. As I started to see and hear them in the same way I began to understand that my life too is sacred text: heaven on earth brought into concrete form.

Your words invited me to open myself to heaven flowing through me into form. I heard the question that lay underneath the words you spoke: "Are [you] ready to graduate from [your] head to [your] heart, from merely appreciating the beauty of creation to actually [recognizing] the music of God's voice playing through it?"[77]

SELECTED PRACTICES TO SUPPORT
READING LIFE AS SACRED TEXT

Two practices, one heart-centered and one head-centered, evolved for me as I learned to read my life as sacred text,. Each prompted me to more mindfully ask "What is Infinite Light and Love saying to me? How is Infinite Light and Love speaking to me through this event or circumstance?

The head-centered practice is a fairly linear five-step practice that is more like reading an already written text. The heart-centered practice, Setting the Stage, is much less linear. It is more like participating in a real time two-way conversation. I found the balance between the two necessary to reading life as sacred text in a meaningful way.

Head-Centered Five-Step Practice. This practice carries a distinct head or mind perspective. It follows a relatively linear process adapted from *lectio divina,* an established Christian practice for reading scripture or other sacred texts.[78] Rather than focusing on scripture or other sacred text, however, it focuses on discerning the presence of Infinite Light and Love in daily experience.

The first step in this practice is to select an event, circumstance, or interaction that stands out, either because it is particularly joyful or especially worrisome. It can be something welcomed or something not welcomed. In this first step I simply attend to the thoughts, experiences, feelings, sights or sounds associated with the event, circumstance, or interaction I've chosen as my focus.

I began using this first step early in my journey to sustaining heaven on earth. While at times it was the wonders of what I was experiencing that most called to me, there were also many times when what most captured my attention was how my life was not playing out as I expected or desired. The nature of what came up did not matter. What did matter was the degree to which it captured my attention.

The second step is to release any judgments or familiar interpretations (e.g., "this was bad," "I should have acted differently") attached to the chosen event or circumstance and allow the experience, be it delight, wonder, miracle, pain, or separation, to exist until the light and love it is made of emerges to illuminate it.[79] As a Buddhist saying puts it: "Do not treasure what is before you; do not reject it; become intimate with it."[80] If, for example, what came up was delightful, I allowed it be delightful without letting fear of its loss diminish that delight. If what came up is not so delightful, I also allowed it to be so. I focused on neither denying nor limiting the presence of Infinite Light and Love, even if hidden. This second step is the springboard to the third.

The third step involved interpreting or "reading" the experience as a communication from Infinite Light and Love. Imagining the event, circumstance, or interaction on which I was focusing as a communication sent to me from the Divine, a visible sign of an invisible reality, I would ask how that might be so and spend time exploring answers as these came to mind. The timing of those answers often had a life of its own. When my mind seemed to be at a loss as to what they might be, I let them arise in their own time from my heart.

One example from my earlier book illustrates how this might work. For a long time, I believed that my friend's repeated admonitions to "Look to God, not me" were meant to turn me away from the "us" I deeply desired. It took much time and reflection using the five steps to understand them differently. When I finally did, though, I realized that they were not said to turn me away from my desired "us." Rather they were said to turn me toward the deeper reality within which our truest "us" drew its shape and strength. Without that reality the "us" I sought would fall short of what it was meant to be.

My response to that interpretation—the subsequent action I took—was in fact the "final" <u>fifth step</u> to my 5-step practice. There is, however, an intervening <u>fourth step</u> I was often tempted to overlook: rest. I so often rushed to action, wanting to know and take the next step in my journey without delay. It took time for me to learn that when I did not allow sufficient time for the results of the third step to "marinate,"[81] the action(s) I took always seemed to fall short. When, instead, I rested and waited, the next right action/response often seemed to take itself.

Though mostly linear the steps were not entirely so. At times when the step I took did not lead me to the sacred text underlying the event, circumstance or interaction I had to take steps back. It was then that I found myself needing to pick up one of the earlier keys before I could move on.

<u>Setting the Stage.</u> I have named the second practice helpful to reading life as sacred text Setting the Stage. It is a less active practice that is, in contrast to the previous one, more heart-based. James Finley's reference to "assuming the inner stance of least resistance" captures the meaning of setting the stage in relation to reading life as sacred text. Finley points out that "The poet cannot make the poem happen, but the poet can assume the inner stance that offers the least resistance to the gift of the poem...lovers cannot force the oceanic oneness, but can assume the inner stance that offers the least resistance to the gift of that."[82]

I was once told that I lived my life at 70mph with my foot on the brake. For a long time I sought to read my life as sacred text in the same way, full speed ahead yet with one eye out for what I could not yet trust or what I still feared might come. St. John of the Cross might say that it is our human faculties—intellect, memory and will—that keep us from "assuming the stance that offers the least resistance." These faculties brake or, more literally, break our receptivity to reading life as sacred text. Our intellect brakes our openness to the hidden aspects of heaven on earth when it jumps in to tell us what the message or meaning of what is before us must be without waiting for its deeper message and meaning to emerge organically.

Memories of past experiences and communications also interfere with our receptivity to the sacred text of our lives in the present. Consciously or unconsciously, they overlay the present with what has happened in the past and what that has meant. They are, for example, quick to remind us of what is no longer present or of how often similar things have gone wrong before and how they may yet go wrong again.

The faculty of our will may be the subtlest yet most powerful brake of all. It pushes us to read our life through the lens of what we want or believe we must have or must do, interpreting any different lens as faulty or threatening.

Releasing the brakes our faculties impose on our receptivity to reading life as sacred text does not, however, mean losing our faculties. That is humanly impossible as well as harmful. What it does mean is switching our faculties from foreground to background so as to no longer allow them to distort or diminish the reality of heaven on earth present in our lives. Until that happens heaven and earth remain in tension rather than in union.

I am still learning to set the stage (i.e., assume my inner stance of least resistance) for reading my life as sacred text. I still struggle to recognize and accept the limitations of my human faculties. Often I continue to read my life in the same way I "listened" to my beloved friend: through the lens of my own thoughts, memories and desires. For a long time, in fact, this tended to be the whole of my practice! Fortunately, as in any human-to-human relationship, the stage does not have to be perfectly set, that it is set as best as possible is always enough.

Book Providence

Bourgeault, C. *Love is Stronger than Death*. This book strongly influenced how I read the sacred in my own life. Bourgeault speaks to the intricate interplay between human and sacred as reflected in the relationship between two beloveds, both while they are physically on earth and when one has passed and the other remains physically on earth. While the scope of my book does not allow for any detailed discussion of this aspect of life's sacred dimension, I feel it's important to reference this one book, which both affirmed for me that I could read life as sacred text and strongly influenced how I did so.

Silver, T. *Outrageous openness: Letting the Divine take the lead* and *It's not your money: How to live fully from Divine abundance*. These books provide multiple concrete examples that illustrate how to read life as sacred text, though those words are not used. While the latter is more specific to money and abundance, it nevertheless offers explicit guidance and steps that can easily be applied to other areas of life.

Bonder, M. *Yiddishe Kop: Creative problem solving in Jewish learning, lore and humor*. This is a delightful though at times frustrating book that explores transcending the limits of what our mind and reason insist is the only possible way to see and interpret life's sacred dimensions. In addition to the realm of logic and reason, Bonder identifies three other realms of reality that are particularly relevant to setting the stage for reading life as sacred text: the hidden realm of the apparent, the apparent realm of the hidden, and the hidden realm of the hidden. Though I have yet to fully understand all of this material, what I have understood has greatly helped me to read my life as sacred text when its alphabet seems most incomprehensible!

Newell, J. P. *Listening to the Heartbeat of God: A Celtic*

Spirituality. A central theme of this book applies directly to reading life as sacred text: "To know the Creator, we need only look at the things...created. ...even what seems to be without vital movement, like the great rocks of earth around us, has within it the light [and love] of God." I found reading it especially helpful in remaining aware of the sacred dimensions of life in general.

Newell, J. P. *The book of creation: An introduction to Celtic spirituality*. Like *Listening to the Heartbeat of God* this book asks, "What does it mean to listen for the Word of God in creation?" The author then takes the reader through each of the days of creation tying each to the concrete expression of Infinite Light and Love within it.

Rohr. R. *Things hidden: Scripture as spirituality*. This book links written scripture and lived experience in deep ways. Rohr describes biblical text in much the same way as the sacred text of our lives might be described, as a "text in travail, struggling toward its conclusions, and only getting the point step by step, and frequently stepping backward.

Valters-Paintner, C. *Eyes of the heart: Photography as a Christian contemplative practice*. In this book Valters-Paintner presents the practice of *visio divina*, a way to view the world around us as sacred text. Her words were the first I'd found that widened the focus of *lectio divina* on scriptural text. They significantly influenced my understanding of life as sacred text.

Benner, D. G. *Opening to God: Lectio divina and life as prayer*. Though specific to prayer and the traditional practice of *lectio divina*, this book helped me flesh out my idea of reading life as sacred text.

Part III
AFTER THOUGHTS

*All God desires is an open heart and a willingness, even
excitement, to see where this Love will take us. God's
relationship with our soul is an 'in-the-moment' affair.*
(A. Farrell)

*H*eaven on earth is not yet fully sustained for me. I am beginning to realize it is not meant to be, at least not in this lifetime. I lived a wondrous love through my adventure of an unexpected friendship with a beloved friend. I am continuing to live that love after his passing. In his physical absence the heaven on earth to which I'd re-awakened and which I've strived to sustain remains, yet it is not as it was nor, I suspect, as it will be. Like in any human relationship sustained over time my relationship with heaven on earth grows and deepens as I become increasingly intimate with its reality.

With that intimacy has come the realization that sustaining heaven on earth is about much more than only the perception and reception of its presence. While that perception and reception was the initial focus that led to the forging of the keys addressed in this book, those keys themselves are now leading me to the awareness that heaven on earth cannot be sustained without being actively lived. Perhaps better said, it cannot be sustained if it is not danced!

The short reflections that follow briefly describe four movements I am finding central to dancing heaven on earth. The first movement is following. Following has been a pervasive movement throughout my adventure. It was following the promise of the love between my friend and I that first led to my experience of the heaven on earth to which it awakened me. That following, in turn, now leads me to follow the dance that is ensuing as I seek to go from only perceiving and receiving heaven on earth to living its reality.

A second movement involves increasing my capacity to receive and sustain the energy of heaven on earth. While the four keys fine-tuned that capacity, dancing to and with that energy now challenges me to shift to what one writer calls a higher "wattage."[83]

As I do I begin to engage with heaven on earth as a fluid reality that engages with me as I engage with it.

Co-creating heaven on earth, the third movement, emerged as the natural outcome of that mutual engagement. An active, reciprocal and intentional partnership with heaven on earth—i.e., dancing—cannot be one-sided, dancing never is. It must be co-created.

There is joy in the dance when it is truly reciprocal and intentional. I became aware of a fourth movement—en-joy-ing—as I filled my lived experience of heaven on earth with joy. En-joy-ing is a movement that in more traditional theological language might be called resting in God's will.[84]

These movements, like the keys, are neither independent nor sequential. They are interdependent and reiterative, flowing in and out like dance steps, dynamic and ever-changing. En-joy-ing, for example, can be understood as a fourth movement flowing out of co-creating, which is how I've framed it. However it can also be understood as a second movement flowing naturally in response to the delight of following heaven on earth.

All four reflections on these movements remain in progress. They are shared here only as a sketch held together by my emerging recognition that what empowers my journey now is its promise of what yet lies ahead, with all its daring and risk.[85] It has been so all along, unending gift.

FOLLOWING

When God's infinite and unconditional love
[i.e., heaven on earth] "seizes your imagination,
[it] will affect everything. ...Fall in love, stay
in love, and it will decide everything."
(Fr. Pedro Arrupe, SJ)

The path that drew me to heaven on earth has always been defined by following. It started with following the pull that recalled me to reconnect with a friend from whom I'd been disconnected for years. It continued as I followed a love that re-awakened me to heaven on earth. It continued further still as I strived to sustain that heaven on earth after my friend's passing. I discovered then that the heaven on earth I sought to sustain was a living reality. Like all living realities it was dynamic and ever-changing, drawing me to follow its music into a deeper love. What was first a following fueled by a personal love gradually morphed into a following defined by what I found at the root of that love: Infinite Light and Love (i.e., heaven on earth). The two, I've discovered, are not so different.

According to one spiritual writer, *talmic* and *talmidim*, the two Aramaic words usually translated as disciple or follower in scripture, carry a much deeper sense of following than typically understood in English. In their Aramaic sense the words are understood to refer to followers so rooted in deep identification and love that what they most desire, what they can't imagine doing without, what animates them and gives them the most pleasure is exactly what animates and directs their following. [86]

Such following is not a following to a destination. It is a following rooted in already being "there," identified with (i.e., one with) the reality followed.[87] When we follow in this sense we become in a way what or whom we love. It is at that level, understood correctly as distinct from dependence,[88] that following personal love and following Infinite Light and Love become one as they did for me.

Writing these words brings to mind a scene from the movie The Princess Bride that can serve as an image of such following, albeit perhaps an imperfect one.[89] It is the scene where the Princess is confronting "the dread pirate Roberts." After berating him, she pushes him down the steep hill on which they are standing. As he is falling, she hears him saying "As you wish." Realizing at those words that he is actually Westley, the friend whose love she has only recently come to recognize, she jumps after him, literally tumbling head over heels to "follow" him to the bottom. It is not a following to get somewhere, it is a following to be *with*.

It is following in this sense upon which I reflect now as I seek to follow rather than only sustain heaven on earth's reality. It is a following that has become what following my love for my friend always was: what I can't imagine doing without, what animates me and gives me the most pleasure—what allows me to dance!

SHIFTING TO A
HIGHER WATTAGE

*[Heaven on earth is always the same], "but we
absorb and reflect it to different degrees. … it's the
wattage of the receiver that makes the difference"*
(D. Brisbin)

*A*s following the love between my friend and me ushered me into an ever-deepening relationship with heaven on earth, my capacity to receive and reflect its reality grew. My spiritual "wattage" shifted to a higher level.[90] The shift happened gradually, almost out of my awareness. At first, I focused on the more concrete benefits of living the love between my friend and me (e.g., companionship, affirmation, courtship). Slowly yet inexorably, the limitations of these benefits became apparent. As they did, less concrete benefits that had been there all along came to the forefront (e.g., a palpable sense of heaven on earth, more joy that I imagined could be). I began to realize that I had been like a 10-watt bulb lugged into a 110-volt socket.[91] My receiving had too often been too limited; my giving primarily a response to it rather than its undeniable mirror.

Heaven on earth is, of course, not more present at the lower levels of wattage where it can be affirmed by sight, hearing and touch. Neither is it less present when those concrete faculties can no longer attest to its presence. What changed for me was my capacity to absorb and reflect it back in return. "Put a lamp on the table and plug it into a 110-volt socket in the wall. Screw in a 15-watt bulb and softly light up the room. Take it out and put in a 100-watt bulb and squint against the glare."[92] Was there more current available to one bulb than the other? No, the source remained 110 volts. Only the bulb's wattage changed.

Just so, I realized, how well and how much I could absorb and consequently dance to the music of heaven on earth depended on my "wattage" (i.e., my openness to its energy). At times when that was low, I could barely hear heaven on earth's music. At other times, when it was higher, I could hear it clearly and easily share in its rhythms.

In keeping with this metaphor, I began to think of heaven on earth's music as streaming through an energetic spectrum that encompassed a range from a "virtually vibration-less awareness of pure consciousness,"[93] which we typically think of as "heaven," to the more solid three-dimensional world of objects, sounds and sights, which we typically think of as "earth."

In reality, of course, it is not so partitioned. Though it may seem that way, the energies of heaven and earth are not discrete, one apart from the other. To loosely adapt words from Barbara Brown Taylor: Where is heaven on earth in this energetic spectrum? It is all over the place, at every level, "revealed in that singular vast net" of energy that animates all that is.[94] When my spiritual wattage was high enough to allow me to plug into the entire spectrum, receiving and giving become one. When I shifted to that higher spiritual wattage, giving became a mirror of the fullness of what I received.

I could receive my friend's love because he first received me! His receiving became gift. As he mirrored me back, unconditionally, without demand or judgment, he slowly led me to learn to do the same. All along while I'd thought I'd been dancing to his giving I'd actually been dancing to his receiving—and then, to receiving heaven on earth sustained.

CO-CREATING
HEAVEN ON EARTH

"...this interplay between the energy flowing from an erotically charged God and that flowing back from an amorous world is the energy that undergirds the very structure of the universe, physical and spiritual"
(R. Rohlheiser)

As I focused on following and shifting to a higher spiritual wattage, I began to discern that dancing to the rhythms of heaven on earth was a co-creative process. The heaven on earth I sought to sustain was not one that came to me pre-packaged, a complete and unchanging reality. Instead it came as a reality whose energy interplayed with my own, engaging with me as I engaged with it. While its notes were pre-formed to express its unique identity, their expression into dance remained yet to be co-created as I heard and interpreted them. The heaven and earth to which I re-awakened through my friend's love invited me—and continues to invite me—to co-create it, to give it substance and weight in my own unique time and space. [95]

Through my dance with heaven on earth I have come to believe that we are each called to be co-creators of the patterns created by the merging of the wondrous mystery of heaven with individual forms here on earth. Heaven on earth is not complete without that intermingling of human and divine identities. Meister Eckhart, a German theologian, philosopher and mystic, poses a thought-provoking question reflective of this understanding: "What good is it to me that Mary gave birth to the son of God fourteen hundred years ago, and I do not also give birth to the Son of God in my time and in my culture? We are all meant to be mothers of God. God is always needing to be born." Another writer has put it this way: "Living between heaven and earth, our job as humans is to bring heaven to earth and earth to heaven, that is to merge the unity and connectedness of heaven with the individual form and function of earth."[96]

The belief of some indigenous communities that we are each born with a unique song in our souls that we are meant to sing affirms this unity and connection. It is a unity and connection that is also echoed in more contemporary writings: "…at the heart of each of us, whatever our imperfections, there exists a silent pulse of perfect rhythm, made up of wave forms and resonances, which is absolutely individual and unique, and yet which connects us to everything in the universe. The act of getting in touch with this pulse can transform our personal experience and in some way alter the world around us."[97]

A perspective closer to my growing image of dance comes from Caryll Houselander who envisions each of us as a hollow reed made to bring "the piper's breath" into form and time. "Are we reed pipes?" he asks, "Is He [Christ] waiting to live lyrically through us?"[98] The image of us as reed pipes awaiting the piper's breath led me to ask: Is heaven on earth waiting for me to allow it to play lyrically through me? How is it inviting me to join in an interactive, dialogic relationship through which Infinite Light and Love gain visible finite form.

The delightful metaphor of a jazz riff that I found recently is expressive of this dialogic aspect of co-creation, which has become so central in both my relationship with my friend and my relationship with heaven on earth. "…God's persuasive love we experience as an evolutionary vibration or impulse within us is like a jazz riff from God that elicits a response from us. We respond with our own riff that may or may not be what God had in mind. Nevertheless, based on what we've played, God responds to our response in a loving way meant to move us to greater love and wholeness.[99]

These metaphors both expand and concretize what I understand as I reflect on and live heaven on earth as a co-created reality, the child of human and divine realities married and becoming one. Like jazz, though, the outcomes of co-creation are always "new, exciting, and unresolved." How they evolve is not and cannot be predetermined.[100] The heaven on earth we each co-create is both the same and uniquely different, like a dance to the same music yet choreographed according to the dancers and the steps chosen.

EN _ JOY _ ING

In Aramaic, God's will is God's sebyana: his desire,
pleasure, delight and deepest purpose. ...The bliss
of Campbell, the desire of Merton, the Kingdom of
Yeshua, the will of the Father are all the same thing—
deepest purpose, desire, pleasure, delight—sebyana.
(D. Brisbin)

The title I've chosen for this movement is meant to convey the contrast between enjoying (without a hyphen), a relatively passive response to a pleasurable experience and en-joying (with a hyphen), a proactive process of intentionally absorbing and embodying the joy of heaven on earth. How well we live heaven on earth is defined first and foremost by our en-joying of it; i.e., by the degree to which we dance to its music.

For a long time, I didn't give much thought to embodying joy intentionally and consistently as an integral aspect of living heaven on earth. I simply enjoyed the experience when it came and yearned desperately for it when it seemed nowhere to be found. Perhaps that was because I found little emphasis on joy as a spiritual practice in Christian spirituality. Crucifixion, suffering, surrender, and sacrifice were all much more prominent emphases. While there is nothing wrong with focusing on these as aspects of spiritual practice, they all to often led me to the misperception of joy as only an occasional gift at best or a terrible distraction at worst.

My understanding of joy as an essential aspect of living heaven on earth rests on my understanding of two words: *will* and *rest*. These words may seem almost contradictory; they had always seemed so to me. Their complementarity, which lies at the core of what I'm calling en-joying, became evident to me as I learned of their meaning from a Middle Eastern perspective.

The first of these words is *sebyana,* the Aramaic word typically translated as "will." From an Aramaic perspective, *sebyana* can also be understood to mean "God's desire, pleasure, delight and deepest purpose."[101] Reflecting on this broader interpretation of "will" changed my understanding of joy radically. Whereas I had previously asked "Am I doing God's will?" (and thought surely that must involve Crucifixion, suffering, surrender, and sacrifice), I began to ask "Am I allowing God's desire, pleasure, delight and deepest purpose to gush forth not only through me but with me and as me?" That question resonated so much more deeply with sustaining and living heaven on earth as I'd come to experience it. More specifically in relation to this fourth movement, I asked "As I seek to sustain and live heaven on earth, to what degree am I en-joying my life; i.e., shaping it according to God's desire, pleasure, delight and deepest purpose?"

Placing my understanding of the word "rest" into its Middle Eastern context further informed my emerging understanding of en-joy-ing as a fourth movement. The meaning of "rest" shifted for me when I read Dan Allender's book *Sabbath* in which he point out how badly we've missed the meaning of rest. According to him the Jewish word for rest can be better translated as "joyous repose, tranquility or delight."

From this perspective, "God didn't rest [on the seventh day] in the sense of taking a nap or chilling out, instead, God celebrated the joy of his creation and sets it free to be connected but separate from the artist."[102] God beholds creation in rapture, with the enjoyment and delight of new parents captivated by the beauty and goodness of their child.[103]

According to Allender we routinely ignore or reject the meaning of rest in this sense because it challenges us to believe the degree to which God truly desires delight and joy for us. He then describes such delight and joy through a metaphor that has stayed with me since I first read it: It is "the kind of delight and joy that would make our silly obsession with work look like futzing over an airline bag of peanuts when outside our window is Mount Rainier in all her winter glory, waiting for the passenger to look and gasp in amazement."

My definition of this fourth movement springs from my revised understanding of both these words: *rest* and *will*. While I've named it "en-joy-ing" it might perhaps be more accurately named "resting in God's will." As I learn to dance to heaven on earth that is both where I start and where I end my dance.

The four keys have taught me to sustain heaven on earth that I might more consistently hear its music. This fourth movement along with the previous three now shapes my dance to the music of its sustained presence.

APPENDIX I

EXCERPT FROM ABBEY OF THE ARTS MONK IN THE WORLD GUEST POST

Isaura Barrera
June 15, 2016

Using the framework of the liturgical hours as a metaphor for the changing facets of my sense of Infinite Light and Love, I've developed a series of reflections in which each "hour" marks the degree to which I am sensing Infinite Light and Love at a given time. It is a practice that helps me both attend to and cultivate the living out of Infinite Light and Love in my daily life. At times, it reminds me that when my sense of Infinite Light and Love is strong I should not cling to it, even as one cannot cling to the sun's bright light at noon. At other times, it reminds me that I need not grieve its passing, for it will once again be strong and even darkness offers unexpected gifts.

Typically, after discerning which "hour" most closely corresponds to my sense of Infinite Light and Love at a given time, I reflect on that hour—what it looks like, what feelings it evokes, its colors and sounds—and on discerning its invitation. If, for example, I do not fully sense Infinite Light and Love yet I can intuit its presence "just around the corner," I imagine a pre-dawn scene. If, on the other hand, my sense of Infinite Light and Love seems to be fading rather than emerging, I imagine a mid-afternoon scene.

REFLECTIONS

Still-hidden Light (Pre-dawn)
Am I filled with a growing sense of Infinite Light and Love gently nudging my darkness aside, giving off glimmers that herald its coming fullness like early birdsong heralds a coming dawn?

> INVITATION: Go forth to the very edges of your longing to receive what waits, wrapped and hidden from sight.

Light on the Horizon (Dawn)
Is my sense of Infinite Light and Love breaking over the horizon of my longing, sending streams of forgotten colors to announce its reawakening?

> INVITATION: Attend to what is being revealed and released from shadow.

Full Light (Mid-morning)
Is my sense of Infinite Light and Love clear, clothing my world with bright colors and ringing sounds?

> INVITATION: Embrace and give thanks for miracles revealed, reclaimed, and re-membered.

Luminous Light (Noon)
Am I filled with a sense of the transcending presence and strength of Infinite Light and Love? (May be a time of wonder or, at times, one that overwhelms, challenging my sense of security and control.)

> INVITATION: Celebrate eternity palpable in finite time and space.

Waning Light and Growing Shadows (Mid-afternoon)
Is my sense of the strength and presence of Infinite Light and Love fading, invaded by growing shadows of shifting feelings, memories, perceptions, and experience?

INVITATION: Listen intently to the continuation of Light's inner music, which never stops even as it becomes less audible, and its dance, which never ends even as it becomes less visible.

Lamp-lighting Time (Evening)

Is my sense of the absence of Infinite Light and Love increasing, erasing the boundaries between light and dark while, paradoxically, simultaneously offering bright splashes of color that pierce the growing darkness?

> INVITATION: Fill your spirit with splashes of color, distilled like honey from the pollen of all that's blossomed in the day.

Darkness (Night)

Is my sense of Infinite Light and Love enveloped in darkness, challenged by the mystery of absence?

> INVITATION: Return the gift of presence to Presence, guided by "no other light than that which burns in your heart" (St. John of the Cross).

Vigil- Keeping Time (Midnight)

Has my sense of the absence of Infinite Light and Love deepened to where even heart's light is having difficulty piercing the darkness?

> INVITATION: Seek intimacy even in absence; tune in to the beloved melody of Infinite Light and Love, waiting like unsung notes to be given voice once again."

APPENDIX II

QUESTIONS FOR FURTHER EXPLORATION OF THE KEYS

(NOTE: The keys can be learned about from another. They are, however, only forged by and for love as embedded in an individual's personal and particular experiences. This appendix is provided as an aid to promoting that forging. It suggests questions that can be asked to probe the keys more directly in relation to readers' experiences. They may be used to explore how the keys may apply to them, as part of further meditation on each of the keys, or merely to stimulate further inspiration.)

Choosing Heaven on Earth Questions

1. Would you say that you have experienced heaven on earth at times? What about those times marked them as heaven on earth for you?

2. What has marked transitions from times you've experienced heaven on earth to times when you did not or could not?

3. Can you identify thresholds, dark nights and bright days in your own experiences? How did these affect your sense of the presence of heaven on earth in your life?

4. Do you believe that you can choose to experience heaven on earth? Have you tried to do so using your imagination when external circumstances did not cooperate?

5. Re-read the distinction between Remembering and re-membering given in Chapter 2 and in Selected Practices for Choosing Heaven on Earth. Are you willing to re-member your past experiences of heaven on earth and in so doing experience them once more as if still present? If not, what keeps you from being willing to do so?

6. Do you believe the key of Choosing Heaven on Earth is being forged in your own life? If so, what do you think is promoting that forging?

DEEPENING LOVE, HOPE AND FAITH QUESTIONS

1. Can you identify times when you've felt you've reached the limits of your ability to love? To hope? To faith?

2. How did you respond to those times?

3. What are your thoughts about the following quote from Thurman re: finding light below the surface light?

    As [the diver] drops deeper and deeper into the abyss, slowly his eyes begin to pick up the luminous quality of the darkness; what was fear is relaxed and he moves into the lower region with confidence and peculiar vision

4. Can you identify times when you found you could go beyond what you believed were the limits of your love? Your hope? Your faith? What do you believe would enabled you or would enable you to do so?

5. Have you thought about or experienced the essence of love, hope, and/or faith that lies beneath and beyond the form in which they are expressed at any given time?

6. Of the practices listed for this key, which might you use the most? Are you familiar with other practices not listed?

7. Do you believe the key of Deepening Love, Hope and Faith is being forged in your own life? If so, what do you think is promoting that forging?

Developing Binocular Vision Questions

1. Have you had times when you've been able to see apparent contradictions as complementary pairs where each supports and adds to the other?

2. How do you believe that your experiences of absence are connected with your experiences of presence? Have you been able to hold both absence and presence together without letting one negate the other? Can you, for example, hold BOTH sorrow at the absence of someone and joy at their presence in your life?

3. How do you believe that your knowing is connected with and related to your unknowing? How much space for unknowing do you allow in your knowing?

4. What contradiction(s), if any, have been the most troublesome for you?

5. Of the practices listed for this key, which might you use the most? Are you familiar with other practices not listed?

6. Do you believe the key of Developing Binocular Vision is being forged in your own life? If so, what do you think is promoting that forging?

READING LIFE AS SACRED TEXT QUESTIONS

1. How do you tend to interpret (i.e., "read") the events in your life (e.g., as signs of what you need to attend to, as possible threats, as blessings)? Can you discern any patterns to your readings?

2. Have you ever asked yourself "How is heaven on earth engaging with me at this time through this experience?" when something has happened? If so, how did you respond?

3. Of the four elements that nurture reading life as sacred text— trust, reciprocity, inclusivity, the act of reading—which do you find easiest? Which most challenging?

4. Of the practices listed for this key, which might you use the most? Are you familiar with other practices not listed?

5. Do you believe the key of Reading Life as Sacred Text is being forged in your own life? If so, what do you think is promoting that forging?

ENDNOTES

1   Anonymous quote found in Lauren Artress' *The path of the holy fool: How the labyrinth ignites our visionary powers*

2   Block, P. (2003). *The answer to how is yes*

3   Google definition

4   Barrera, I. (2019) *Unwrapping beloved's gift, Co-creating soul's song: Way stations on the way to co-creating soul's song*

5   Ibid

6   personal translation based on Spanish version in Barnstone, 1972

7   In my earlier book I discuss why, despite its centrality to my adventure, I do not focus on the details of this friendship. As I said in that book: "I know now that my journey was and continues to be defined not by the particularities of a single friendship but by the process of opening to and reclaiming [the heaven on earth] to which that friendship reawakened me."

8   I share my reflections on how that adventure awakened me to heaven on earth in my earlier book: *Unwrapping Beloved's Gift, Co-Creating Soul's Song: Way Stations on the Path to Awakening Deep Love, Hope and Faith*

9   Literally, "each head a world"

10 See Pannikar, R. *The experience of God* for further discussion of this understanding.

11 Over time I also came to experience heaven on earth during times of fear, doubt, confusion and dreams unfulfilled, but that was not initially so

12 Booram, B. A. & Booram, D. *When faith becomes sight: Opening your eyes to God's presence all around you*

13 Ibid

14 Philip, L. M. *The discerning heart: The developmental psychology of Robert Kegan*

15 Ibid

16 I use the term Infinite Light and Love in place of other terms such as God, Source, or the Divine to emphasize the essence of heaven on earth and avoid misconceptions and misperceptions attached to those terms.

17 Bob Holmes, in Virtual Abbey Facebook post, 11/15/19

18   Bourgeault, C. (2008) *Love is stronger than death: The mystical union of two souls*

19   Newell, J. P. *Christ of the Celts: The healing of creation.*

20   Vaughn-Lee, L. (2011). *Fragments of a love story: Reflections from the life of a mystic.*

21   This fact, long affirmed by spiritual writers, is now being increasingly affirmed by science (e.g., recognition that dark matter, a form of matter that cannot be directly detected, makes up approximately 85% of the matter in the universe). See also writers such as Ilia Delio and Barbara Fiand, who both speak to the convergence of science and spirituality.

22   Based on definition given by Newell, J. P. (*Remembering the past, remembering the future.* Huffington Post, 11/9/2011)

23   This is my interpretation based on several internet references on the Jewish understanding of remembrance

24   When Mary Magdalene met Jesus in the garden after his death, she did not meet a memory. She met a living Jesus restored to wholeness.

25   Chopra, D. (2019). *Metahuman*

26   This practice is addressed further in subsequent chapters

27   Boss, G. (2016). *All creation waits: The Advent mystery of new beginnings.*

28   It's important to note that my understanding of dark nights is my own though deeply influenced by St. John of the Cross as well as R. Rolhieser, who introduced me to my formal study of St. John's work at the Oblate School of Theology.

29   The analogy of sight is an imperfect and limited one. Dark nights obscure what we perceive regardless of the senses involved. Readers are invited to substitute the sense that feels most comfortable to them.

30   Bourgeault, C. *Mystical Hope*

31   Ibid

32   Shulman, J. (2006). *The instruction manual for receiving God*

33   Barrera, I. (2019). *Unwrapping beloved's gift, Co-creating soul's song: Way stations on the path to awakening deep love, hope and faith.*

34   One version of this story can be found in the Preface to *Gates of the forest* by Elie Weisel

35   I say the following about this in my earlier book: "the characters in these [sciipture] stories possessed what I so deeply and desperately longed for: a sense of gifted love so strong and so deep it quite literally brings heaven to earth…"

36   Steindl-Rast, D. & Lebell, S. (2001). *Music of silence: A sacred journey through the hours of the day.*

[37] This section lists selected resources that I found through what Carolyn Gratton calls "book providence," the experience of having just the right book fall into your awareness seemingly out of nowhere.

[38] Faith is used here as a verb

[39] Thurman, H. (2014). *The luminous darkness*

[40] Adapted from C. Bourgeault, *Wisdom Way* 2003. Original statement reads as follows: "soul energy released in the sacrifice reveals the name of God I truly bear while at the same time making it available as a fragrance and a nutrient." I believe that it is through this that we ultimately receive the answers that we seek.

[41] Salzberg, S. (2003). *Faith: Trusting Your Own Deepest Experience*, p.81. Riverhead Books

[42] Ibid. Cynthia Bourgeault also talks about the essence of hope in her book, *Mystical hope.*

[43] Rohr, R. Weekly Meditation

[44] Finley, J. *Turning to Teresa of Avila.* In Action for Action and contemplation's Turning to the Mystics podcast series

[45] Bourgeault, C. (2016). *The heart of centering prayer: Nondual Christianity in theory and practice*

[46] Ibid

[47] Ryan, Lines from introductory poem

[48] In her book on the *Heart of Centering Prayer*, Cynthia Bourgeault identifies "putting the mind in the heart" as a phrase from the *Philokalia*, "that hallowed collection of spiritual writings from the Christian East."

[49] Bourgeault, C. (2016). *The heart of Centering prayer: Nondual Christianity in theory and practice*

[50] Rohr, R. Daily *Changing Places*, Daily meditation for November 15, 2019

[51] Paraphrased from Shaia, A. *Beyond the Biography of Jesus: The Journey of Quadratos* Book II

[52] Barrera, I. & Kramer, L. (2017). *Skilled dialogue: Authentic communication and collaboration across diverse perspectives*

[53] Barrera, I. (2019). *Unwrapping beloved's gift, co-Creating soul's song; Way stations on the way to co-creating soul's song*

[54] These contradictions and my struggles with them are discussed in *Unwrapping beloved's gift, co-Creating soul's song.* The discussion in this book focuses more specifically on how they are affected by the use of binocular vision.

[55] Barrera, I. (2019). *Unwrapping beloved's gift, co-creating soul's song:*

56   Adapted from a discussion of non-duality in C. Bourgeault's *The heart of centering prayer: Nondual Christianity in theory and practice.*

57   While many if not most cultural conditioning and scripts once affirmed binocular vision (i.e., non-duality), that affirmation diminished, practically disappearing in Western cultures as science gained prominence. Only relatively recently is its role as a key to opening our perception of the world as more than a nucleated object apart from all that is not concrete and three-dimensional being once again recognized and promoted. See, for example, D. Chopra's discussion of in his book *Metahuman,* as well as I. Delio's brilliant synthesis of theological and scientific perspectives in her book *The unbearable wholeness of being.*

58   Barrera, I. & Kramer, L. (2017). *Skilled dialogue: Authentic communication and collaboration across diverse perspectives,* for example.

59   Zander, R. S. & Zander, B. *The art of possibility: Transforming professional and personal life*

60   Seelig, T. (2012). *inGenius: A crash course on creativity*

61   See www.thework.org

62   The four questions can be found at www.thework.org. My discussion of them here is based on my understanding and application of them. It is intended only for purposes of their use in the practice of supporting binocular vision and not to give directions to their general use.

63   Spiritual reality tends to acquire a deeper reality when someone we love deeply passes. While neither the scope nor the intent of this book allow for further discussion of this, readers who wish more information are referred to *Love Is Stronger then Death* by Cynthia Bourgeault as well as other sources listed in Book Providence.

64   Silver's questions delightfully reframe what has more traditionally been phrased as the discernment of God's will (i.e., heaven on earth). Readers are referred to books referenced in the Providence section for further exploration of this understanding.

65   Rohr, R. Online meditation (12/21/2020)

66   See J. Philip Newell's *Listening for the heartbeat of God* and *The book of creation.*

67   Newell, P. (1999). *The book of creation: Introduction to Celtic spirituality*

68   Taken from Rob Brezny's definition of pronoia as "the suspicion that the whole world is conspiring to shower you with blessings."

69   Quote is taken from Teilhard de Chardin's marvelous little book *How I believe* (1969) in which he talks about "superpersonalization" and the completion of unity through diversity.

70 See discussion on heaven on earth in Part I for further discussion of this point

71 Paraphrase of quote from Rilke cited by Cynthia Bourgeault in *Love stronger than death*. Original quote reads as follows: "Perhaps all the dragons in our lives are princesses who are only waiting to see us act, just once, with beauty and courage."

72 The role that ego, our "homemade self," plays in our interpretation of others' actions becomes glaringly clear after someone passes and one-half of a human relationship is no longer active for us to push for or against.

73 There are other models. For example, St. Ignatius, a 15th century mystic proposed a dichotomy more focused on subjective experience: consolation and desolation. I've chosen to focus only on Silver's dichotomy because it more clearly reflects my emphasis on relationship.

74 Rilke, R. M. (1993). *Letters to a young poet*

75 A paradoxical statement used in Buddhist practices to train monks to go beyond dependence on reason and logic and open to intuitive non-rational insights (e,g., What is the sound of one hand clapping?). A similar admonition is given in St Ignatius' Spiritual Exercises in regard to making decisions.

76 Rabbi Milton Bonder names three such dimensions or realms in his book *Yiddishe Kop: Creative problem-solving in Jewish learning, lore and humor*: the hidden realm of what is apparent, the apparent realm of what is hidden, and the hidden realm of what is hidden.

77 Brisbin, D. *Daring to think again: Restoring Jesus' original challenge to the faith we think we know*

78 Readers are referred to sources listed in Book Providence for more specific discussion of this tradition as typically practiced. The five-step practice adapts this practice specifically in relation to my adventure and the purposes of this book.

79 I first encountered this idea of allowing delight, wonder, miracle, pain, or separation to exist until the light and love they are made of emerges to illuminate and transform our perspective in Shulman, J.'s *The instruction manual for receiving God*

80 Buddhist teaching told to me by a friend (thanks, Trudy)

81 Thanks for this wonderful image, Rachel Slagle Pearson

82 Taken from a frequently cited quote from one of Finley's presentations/teachings

83 D. Brisbin uses this metaphor, which is discussed more specifically in the second reflection

84   See discussion of the Aramaic understanding of God's will and of rest in the reflection on this movement

85   Living that promise in the present is key.

86   Brisbin, D. *Daring to think again: Restoring Jesus' original challenge to the faith we think we know.*

87   As I write this I realize that this understanding of following is one that unfortunately can be most readily understood negatively. It is easy, for example, to see an addict identified with and loving his or her drug of choice. Understanding following positively in its Aramaic sense as a reflection of authentic love seems to be both less common and more challenging. I wonder if perhaps this reveals a bias toward according more power to evil than good, or perhaps merely reveals the emphasis placed on independence in Western cultures.

88   Following rooted in deep love is never about becoming dependent on what or whom one loves. That would betray love's deepest truth, its unconditional quality.

89   Scene can be found on YouTube under the heading Princess Bride As You Wish. The movie as a whole can be seen as a great exemplar of following understood in a positive sense.

90   The metaphor of spiritual wattage is used D. Brisbin in his book *Daring to think again: Restoring Jesus' original challenge to the faith we think we know.*

91   Ibid

92   From D. Brisbin, *Daring to think again: Restoring Jesus' original challenge to the faith we think we know.*

93   C. Bourgeault. *The wisdom way of knowing: Reclaiming an ancient tradition to awaken the heart.*

94   B. Brown Taylor. *The luminous web: Essays on science and religion.* Original passage reads "Where is god in this picture? God is all over the place. God is up there, down here, inside my skin and out. God is the web, the energy, the space, the light—not captured in them, as if any of these concepts were more real than what unites them—but revealed in that singular vast net of relationships that animates everything that is."

95   The notion of co-creating heaven on earth is not a new. It is also not a notion meant to diminish or blur the distinction between Creator and created. Rather it is one within which the identities of each are acknowledged and honored.

96   Brisbin, D. *Daring to think again: Restoring Jesus' original challenge to the faith we think we know.*

[97] Leonard, G. (2006) *The silent pulse: A search for the perfect rhythm that exists in each of us*

[98] Caryll Houselander, *The reed of God.*

[99] Steve Hansen, *Jazz, evolution, and co-creation with trinity,* www.omegacenter.info (3/4/2019)

[100] Ibid

[101] D. Brisbin (2019). *Daring to think again: Restoring Jesus' original challenge to the faith we think we know*

[102] D. B. Allender (2010). *Sabbath: The ancient practices*

[103] Ibid

Printed in the United States
by Baker & Taylor Publisher Services